The
Margaret Palca
★ BAKES ★
Cookbook

The Margaret Palca
★ BAKES ★
Cookbook

80 Cakes, Cookies, Muffins, and More from a Famous Brooklyn Baker

Margaret Palca
Photography by Michael Harlan Turkell

Skyhorse Publishing

Copyright © 2018, 2021 by Margaret Palca
Photography © 2018 by Michael Harlan Turkell

Skyhorse Publishing books may be purchased in bulk at special discounts for sales promotion, corporate gifts, fund-raising, or educational purposes. Special editions can also be created to specifications. For details, contact the Special Sales Department, Skyhorse Publishing, 307 West 36th Street, 11th Floor, New York, NY 10018 or info@skyhorsepublishing.com.

Skyhorse® and Skyhorse Publishing® are registered trademarks of Skyhorse Publishing, Inc.®, a Delaware corporation.

Visit our website at www.skyhorsepublishing.com.

10 9 8 7 6 5 4 3 2 1

Library of Congress Cataloging-in-Publication Data is available on file.

Cover design by Daniel Brount with special thanks to Katie Kalin
Cover photograph by Michael Harlan Turkell

Hardcover ISBN: 978-1-5107-3267-4
Paperback ISBN: 978-1-5107-5626-7
Ebook ISBN: 978-1-5107-3268-1

Printed in China

This book is dedicated to my brilliant, beautiful, clever, thoughtful, and devoted mother, Doris Caryl Wilk Palca— with all my love and gratitude.

TABLE OF CONTENTS

FOREWORD

My sister was not supposed to be a baker.

She was supposed to pursue a career in some art-related profession—possibly a curator or an art historian or art publisher. She even worked for a time at an art institute, so everyone in the family was a bit taken aback when Margaret left that job to work as an apprentice baker in a fancy food shop in Manhattan.

I guess we shouldn't have been surprised. Margaret would spend endless hours with our grandmother making cookies, jelly rolls, and something Grandma always referred to as "those bars you love," a three-layered affair with a plain cookie base, chocolate chip middle, and coconut on top. We both liked these bars, but neither Margaret nor I were entirely sure why Grandma had determined that these were my favorite. I might point out here that Grandma never asked me if I wanted to bake anything with her. (She did, however, allow me once to help her make chopped chicken liver, and to this day I can't chop an onion without thinking of that experience.)

One of the things that impresses me most about my sister's baking is her commitment to excellence. "Good enough" is never good enough for Margaret. Recipes that call for butter get butter, not lower cost margarine. There's a right way to make her signature rugelach dough, and a wrong way. It's always the right way for Margaret.

At the same time Margaret never gives me the impression that baking is a magical art to be mastered only by a select few. One time I needed to bring a dessert to a party, and I asked Margaret what I should make. She sent me the recipe for her remarkably simple carrot cake. I followed her directions, and produced a dessert that was sublime, quite to the astonishment of my friends. I'd say that even a clod in the kitchen like me can get it right with Margaret's directions.

But if baking is straightforward, it is still not something to be trifled with. Hedge fund managers or TV celebrities who decide to try a new challenge by becoming bakers drive my sister nuts. When they produce glitzy cookbooks sharing their newly discovered secrets, Margaret just shakes her head. For my sister, baking always presents new challenges— maybe making her own sourdough starter and creating magnificent rolls, maybe concocting a recipe for whoopee pies—but baking is never a "new challenge." It's the only challenge.

I'm so proud of my sister's success as a baker, and so happy this book will let her share her years of baking wisdom with others. You can decide for yourself if her coconut bars deserve the title of "those bars you love." But if they don't do that for you, that's okay—another recipe in this book certainly will.

—Joe Palca, science correspondent for NPR
(and Margaret's brother)

INTRODUCTION

I have an early memory as a little girl standing on a chair in my Grandma's tiny kitchen in her beautiful New York City apartment. This extraordinary woman was an accomplished pianist, an art collector, well read, a plant lover, as well as a natural born baker—a talent she liked to share with me. I couldn't wait for our dates. Often, she would let me watch her make blintzes, and her yeast coffee cake was celebrated but too complicated for an afternoon visit, so we usually stuck to chocolate chip cookies (pg. 10) and Santa Snacks (pg. 13)—licking of little fingers was always compulsory. Her old hands never lost their skill.

My next excursion into the food world took place in high school. As seniors, we were given a six-week work period to explore different professions, so our families opened their offices and businesses and shared them with the class. I wanted to work in a restaurant and was lucky enough to find a spot in one of the most elegant French restaurants in New York: Le Pavillon. The pastry chef known as Willy took me under his wing, shared his techniques, and introduced me to the walk-in refrigerator. I had never seen so many quarts of heavy cream. After separating eggs for hours and hours, Willy would reward me with a small version of that night's special dessert—once a Grand Marnier soufflé. The best part of the job was taking home samples. Even my Grandma was impressed.

Willy and me at Le Pavillon

After my taste of French cuisine in New York, I was anxious to see the real thing so I persuaded my parents to send me to Paris the summer before college. Paris, what a wonderful city to be in if you love food—and pastry. For two months, I studied French at the Alliance Francais and cooking at École de Cuisine Le Pot au Feu.

Then came college and the trauma of the newly independent years. I was laid off from my first job at the American Federation of Arts and thought *now what? Could I possibly be a baker, what I really yearned for?* It began to take shape in my mind. I had a notion that to be professional I had to create a product most people wouldn't make at home. I decided on the madeleine, a small shell-shaped sponge cake made famous by Marcel Proust. It turned out to be a temperamental little so-and-so with clarified butter, well-sifted flour, and everything at just the right temperature. I tested every version of the recipe I could find until I arrived at the perfect madeleine. My father, my champion who believed I could do anything, offered to be my sales agent but I was much too scared. Off he went anyway to deliver my samples to Joel Dean, the owner of the then-brand-new and elegant Dean & DeLuca in Soho. Mr. Dean loved it and ordered six dozen.

Quick recognition was good for my ego, but it takes a lot of madeleines to pay the rent so I went to work at a fancy gourmet shop on the Upper East Side of Manhattan called Fraser Morris Fine Foods, but only part-time. I apprenticed myself to Russell Carr, the pastry chef for the Chelsea Baking Company. After finishing my morning shift at Fraser Morris, I would head downtown to work with Russell. He taught me how to roll and make pie dough and various fillings. He was also a masterful decorator—he could make icing roses the size of a pin. His techniques were an inspiration to me.

When the owners of Fraser Morris saw how serious I was about baking, they allowed me to sell some of my baked goods in the shop. Pretty soon, because of their success, they asked me to be full-time baker for the shop. and put a professional kitchen at my disposal—I couldn't have been happier! For three years I baked nonstop, winning the hearts of the Upper East Side neighborhood.

With this invaluable experience under my belt, I felt that it was time to be my own boss, so I left Fraser Morris and went back to baking at home in Manhattan. A friend recommended some coffee shops on Court Street in Brooklyn that might be prospective customers, so in 1984 with sample products under my arm, I took the #2 train to Borough Hall in Brooklyn, walked down Court Street, and found not only new customers but a lifestyle that suited me. I persuaded my family to rent a large Brooklyn brownstone and converted the entire basement into a huge kitchen.

The house was on a quiet street and the smells from the rugelach we baked were irresistible to the neighbors. We soon had friends. By coincidence there was a restaurant supply factory at the end of the block. The factory workers would hang around my door looking longingly at the cookies. My reward for the samples I gave them was a huge oval metal cookie platter I use to this day. And so my bakery became a reality. I called it Margaret Palca Bakes so there would be no question about what I do or who I am.

When the original Brooklyn brownstone was no longer available, my husband and I packed up our equipment, daughters, and cats and moved westward across the vast plains of the Brooklyn-Queens Expressway (BQE) into no-man's-land. This no-man's-land is now known as Brooklyn's exclusive Columbia Street Waterfront District, but this was not the case in 1989. With rundown buildings, huge vacant lots inhabited by rats and garbage, we were pioneers, but the poor condition of the neighborhood made it possible for us to afford a house with a perfect view of the Manhattan skyline from the third story window. Plus, the first floor of the house was a commercial space—perfect for a bakery. My former boss at Fraser Morris gave me all the bakery equipment that was no longer in use after my departure. What a windfall. Two mixers, bowls, sheet pans and racks, the works (and all free) and we were really in business.

For almost eight years I baked in this house. We sold hundreds of pounds of rugelach per week; we couldn't roll it fast enough. Our customers were all the major food shops in Manhattan: Balducci's, Dean & DeLuca, Jefferson Market, Citarella Gourmet Market, Garden of Eden Marketplace, Amish Market, Mangia, Fairway Market, and lots of smaller cafés. My father was very proud. Rugelach was no longer our only attraction. We added a whole repertoire of baked goods and were constantly coming up with new recipes and filling requests for loaf cakes, fruit tarts, red velvet cupcakes, cream cheese brownies, pecan bars, and more.

As with our first Brooklyn neighborhood, we made our presence felt in this neighborhood, too. Marty Markowitz, Brooklyn Borough President, gave me a certificate from his office declaring an official Margaret Palca Bakes day. The men in the "social club" across the street didn't know what to make of me. "No Italian cannolis?" We put an espresso machine in the tiny café in front of our kitchen so that my "minimob" could have a place to sit with espresso—and rugelach.

Marty Markowitz and me at Margaret Palca Bakes

In 1989, food writer Ed Levine "discovered" me. His article about his search for the best rugelach appeared in the *New York Times*—and I was featured! It is a truly exciting and flattering experience to open the newspaper and see a picture of yourself. Not to mention the extraordinary reach of the *New York Times*. The phone rang for days and from places as far away as Minnesota.

We were bursting at the seams until it came time to expand once more to our present location. The landlord was thrilled to rent me the space when we first moved in—it

New York Times feature, November 12, 1997

had been vacant for a long time. We are now on Columbia Street in Brooklyn with a huge kitchen, bakery, and small café facing the street. I'm able to accommodate more equipment (with my own walk-in refrigerator!) plus more man power than I've ever had before. By now I am known in the neighborhood. Our café attracts old friends and newcomers alike. I've made birthday cakes for children who are now asking me to bake their wedding cakes.

The café in front of the bakery needed a range of new food offerings besides baked goods. Sandwiches, for instance. But what bread to use? A baker faced with this dilemma has to roll up her sleeves and create her own rolls (with some help from Nancy Silverton of La Brea Bakery and Amy from Amy's Bread by my side). I am now a bread baker and the mother of a sour dough starter, scientific wonder child.

For as long as I've been baking, I am still learning. Food trends change and you have to accommodate. There are now chia and flax seeds in my whole wheat bread. Who would have thought that roasted kale bread crumbs would catch on? How do you make breakfast oatmeal so delicious you can't wait to eat it? Bake it with lots of dried fruits and nuts—and keep it gluten-free in the bargain. This book is a kind of cooking memoir—a chronological guide to my baking career and all the recipes that led me to Margaret Palca Bakes. The index will guide you in a more traditional way. I'm pleased to share these baking secrets with you along with everything else I've learned over my thirty-five-year culinary journey.

BASIC EQUIPMENT

- ★ Measuring spoons
- ★ Liquid and dry measuring cups (preferably not made of glass)
- ★ Spatulas
    - ★ Large and small rubber spatulas
    - ★ A flat metal spatula and an offset metal spatula
- ★ Large plastic bowl scraper
- ★ Dough hook, paddle, and whisk attachments for your mixer
- ★ Food Processor
- ★ Metal bowls of many sizes (plus one bigger than you think you'll ever use)
- ★ Heavy bottomed cookie sheets and baking pans
- ★ Parchment paper and pan release spray (this is indispensable)
- ★ Rolling pins (match the size of your pin to the size of the work space)
    - ★ A traditional rolling pin (good for sugar and gingerbread dough)
    - ★ A French tapered wooden pin (good for rolling pie dough and rugelach rounds)
- ★ Sturdy pot holders
- ★ Pastry bags and couplers with various sized tips
- ★ Food coloring, decorations, and sprinkles
- ★ Space in your refrigerator and freezer
- ★ A digital food scale (can be useful, but not essential)

Helpful Hints

Read each recipe carefully before you start. It's important to have all the ingredients, but you can make some substitutions. You can use brown sugar in place of granulated sugar by adding an extra ¼ cup of brown sugar. You can create buttermilk out of whole milk by adding 1 tablespoon of lemon juice to 1 cup of whole milk. You can also substitute sour cream for buttermilk in the exact amounts.

Plan in advance. Many ingredients must be used at room temperature. Some need to be kept chilled. This is indicated in every recipe.

Don't leave the room while you're baking. Your oven may not bake evenly and you might need to move the pan to a higher or lower rack during baking. I give an average range of baking times but it is advisable to check the oven often.

General Observations

Baking is messy work. You wash your hands every five minutes (forget beautiful nails), you dirty a lot of equipment, and the equipment you dirty won't always fit in the dishwasher. One great advantage of being a professional baker is . . . someone else washes the dishes.

Rolling dough takes practice. Overworked dough, rolled, and rerolled will be tough. It is better to settle for an imperfect round than to reroll it.

Always make rugelach on a cool, dry day. The cooler the room the better.

Pie dough is a fragile dough. Do not reroll it or the crust will be too doughy. Throw away the scraps of leftover dough when rolling pie or tart shells.

Scraps of sugar and linzer dough can be reused.

Be very gentle with yeast dough. If you are having a hard time forming rolls, let the dough rest. Leave it for ten minutes on the floured work table and drape a piece of plastic wrap over it. It will be easy to form again. This will take practice. The bread will taste delicious even if it doesn't look perfect. You can mist the rolls while they're baking. Halfway through baking I spray the rolls with water to create steam to give them somewhat more of a crust.

Using a pastry bag also requires practice. Some people get the feel of the bag right away and others find the icing coming out of the top. The pastry bag can get clogged, but running the tip under very hot water while you squeeze the bag usually does the trick. If not, take off the tip of the bag and wash it. You must stir the icing well before filling the pastry bag.

A Final Thought

I have always tried not to be wasteful of ingredients or even the finished product. I don't believe in disposable pans or pastry bags. I try to recycle my garbage bags from one bread baking to the next. If you have made too large a batch of baked goods, find someone you can share with.

CHAPTER ONE

WHAT I LEARNED FROM GRANDMA

CHOCOLATE CHIP COOKIES

▪▪

I love chocolate chip cookies. I believe a chocolate chip cookie a day keeps the doctor away. I loved making chocolate chip cookies with my grandma and eating the delicious batter—I couldn't wait for the cookies to come out of the oven. If you feel the same way about chocolate chip cookies, I recommend making enough dough to bake a batch of cookies plus extra to store in the refrigerator for later so that whenever you need a cookie, it is only a few minutes away.

MAKES 24–30 COOKIES

1 cup unsalted butter at room temperature
¾ cup granulated sugar
¾ cup brown sugar
2 extra-large eggs
½ tsp. pure vanilla extract

2 cups all-purpose flour
1 tsp. baking soda
¼ tsp. salt
⅓ cup chopped walnuts
2 cups semi-sweet chocolate chips

Preheat oven to 350°F. Spray a cookie sheet or line it with parchment paper. In the bowl of an electric mixer beat the butter and sugars at medium speed until well combined. Break the eggs into a cup and add them to the mixer followed by the vanilla. Measure the flour, baking soda, and salt into a small bowl and add to the mixer, beating on low speed until the flour is combined. Add the walnuts and chocolate chips and mix until combined. If the dough is very soft, chill it for 30 minutes. Form the dough into balls about the size of a ping pong ball. Eight should fit on a 10 x 15-inch cookie sheet and give the cookies room to spread. Bake for 10 to 12 minutes or until cookies are lightly brown. Remove from oven and allow the cookies to cool so you don't burn your mouth! Use all the dough or place in a plastic container. Store in the refrigerator for up to 2 weeks or in the freezer for up to 3 months.

SANTA SNACKS OR MAGIC BARS

▪▪

These delicious bars were always our favorites to make because we loved nibbling on the ingredients as we added them. We made them all year round (despite their name).

MAKES 9 BARS

½ cup unsalted butter, melted

1 cup flaked coconut

1 cup graham cracker crumbs

1 cup semi-sweet chocolate chips

1 cup chopped nuts

1 (15 oz.) can sweetened condensed milk

Preheat oven to 350° F. Spray a 9 x 9 x 2-inch baking pan. Combine butter, coconut, and graham cracker crumbs in baking pan. Press lightly. Cover with a layer of semi-sweet chocolate chips. Sprinkle with a layer of chopped nuts. Drizzle sweetened condensed milk evenly over the surface. Bake for 25 to 30 minutes or until lightly brown and bubbly on top. Cool completely before cutting.

CHAPTER TWO

MY FIRST PRODUCT

MADELEINES

17

MADELEINES

▪▪

I wanted to be a professional baker, but I only had a home oven at my disposal. I needed to think hard about what product would be my introduction. I came up with madeleines because I had inherited several madeleine pans and loved how they looked, so I set out to perfect the recipe. I was fortunate to have a father who didn't mind testing my unsuccessful first attempts of batches that were too dry, too hard, too rubbery! Until finally a perfect, delicate madeleine came to life. Keep in mind that you must eat them fast; their delicate cake quality is fleeting—like the madeleine business.

MAKES 24 MADELEINES

2 extra-large eggs
⅓ cup granulated sugar
Rind of ½ a lemon
1 tsp. pure vanilla extract

5 tbsp. unsalted melted butter, clarified*
½ cup all-purpose flour

Preheat oven to 350°F. Spray two madeleine pans. In the bowl of an electric mixer beat eggs and sugar until light and fluffy, add the lemon rind, and vanilla and beat to combine. Remove the bowl from the machine. Add butter and flour alternately and fold them in gently with a rubber spatula so you do not deflate the eggs. No flour lumps or butter lines should be visible. With a spoon, fill the madeleine pans and place them in the oven. Bake 5 to 7 minutes. You must watch carefully as they bake very fast and you do not want them to brown. Allow to cool for a few minutes. It is easier to remove them from the pan when they are still slightly warm. Lift the madeleine pan on its side and with a small knife loosen the madeleine at the base of the shell. It should fall out. Allow to cool completely on a metal rack. Sprinkle with confectioners' sugar and eat within 24 hours.

---

* To clarify the butter, melt it in to a small saucepan and remove any of the white foamy bits that float to the top. You want a pure yellow liquid.

CHAPTER THREE
FRASER MORRIS

BLUEBERRY MUFFINS

▰▱

These have always been the most popular muffin I make. The inspiration for this recipe came from Gourmet magazine, once the most popular and perhaps only cooking magazine available. Of the many thousands of muffins I've made over the years, I have personally stirred by hand practically every blueberry muffin sold in my bakery.

MAKES 10–11 MUFFINS

2½ cups quick oats

1½ cups buttermilk

1½ cups brown sugar

4 extra-large eggs

1 cup unsalted butter, melted

2 cups all-purpose flour

1 tbsp. baking powder

½ tsp. salt

2 cups fresh or frozen blueberries

Preheat oven to 350°F. Spray a 12-muffin (½-cup capacity) pan. These muffins are very difficult to remove from the pan, so be sure you have sprayed the muffin cups very well. In a large bowl combine quick oats and buttermilk. Then add brown sugar, eggs, and melted butter. Stir well to break up any brown sugar lumps. Add flour, baking powder, and salt. Stir well. Fold in blueberries and fill muffin cups to completely full. You may get only 10 or 11 muffins. Place in oven and bake 35 to 40 minutes or until muffins are brown on top. Allow to cool completely. A suggestion for removing the muffins: place pan on its side and gently tap it on the counter. This will loosen the muffins. Muffins taste best the day they are baked.

BANANA MUFFINS

When the bananas in your fruit bowl are all turning brown, this is the perfect time to make banana muffins. The riper the banana the sweeter the muffin.

MAKES 6–7 MUFFINS

2 ripe bananas
1 cup granulated sugar
2 extra-large eggs
½ cup unsalted butter, melted
½ cup sour cream

1½ cups all-purpose flour
1 tsp. baking soda
½ tsp. salt
½ cup chopped walnuts

Preheat oven to 350°F. Spray a 12-muffin (½-cup capacity) pan. Purée the bananas in a food processor and pour into a large bowl. Add all the rest of the ingredients and stir well to combine (do not worry about overbeating). The batter will be rather thin, making it easy to pour directly into the prepared cups. Lift the bowl and guide the batter slowly into the cups with a spatula. Fill cups completely. You will get 6 or 7 muffins from this recipe. Bake for 20 to 25 minutes or until well browned. Allow to cool completely. Muffins taste best the day they are baked.

APPLE CRUMB MUFFINS

Anything with sour cream, chopped apples plus crumbs on top sounds delicious to me. If you want to make these muffins for breakfast, chop the apples the night before, toss them with a teaspoon of lemon juice, and store them in the refrigerator until the morning.

MAKES 6–7 MUFFINS

Muffins:

¼ cup granulated sugar

2 extra-large eggs

¼ cup unsalted butter, melted

1 cup sour cream

1 apple, peeled, cored, chopped (add 1
    tsp. lemon juice if storing overnight)

1½ cups all-purpose flour

2 tsp. baking powder

¼ tsp. baking soda

¼ tsp. salt

½ tsp. cinnamon

Crumb topping:

1 cup walnuts

½ cup granulated sugar

½ cup all-purpose flour

½ tsp. cinnamon

2 tbsp. unsalted butter, chilled

Make the muffins:
Preheat oven to 350°F. Spray a 12-muffin (½-cup capacity) pan. Combine all ingredients in a large bowl and stir well to combine. Spoon batter into muffin cups. You should have 6 to 7 muffins.

Make the topping:
Place all crumb topping ingredients into the bowl of a food processor. With the metal blade, pulse the mixture until it reaches a crumbly texture. Do not overmix or you will end up with a wet blob. Sprinkle the crumbs on top of the muffins and press them down gently. Place muffins in oven and bake for 20 to 25 minutes or until lightly brown on top and firm in the center. Allow to cool completely. If you have leftover crumbs, save them in the refrigerator for next time. Muffins taste best the day they are made but they can be frozen for up to 3 months.

CRANBERRY MUFFINS

▪▪

When I first opened the café, I thought I should make every kind of muffin that was asked for. I still do, but each of my muffins has a distinct personality and a following. My bakery regulars Noon and Rob have come almost every day since I opened on President Street in 1989 to buy their cranberry muffins for breakfast. I thank them for their loyalty.

MAKES 5–6 MUFFINS

1 cup granulated sugar

½ cup unsalted butter, melted

½ cup milk

2 extra-large eggs

1½ cups all-purpose flour

1 tsp. baking powder

½ tsp. salt

½ cup chopped walnuts

2 cups chopped cranberries

Preheat oven to 350°F. Spray a 12-muffin (½-cup capacity) pan. Combine all ingredients except the cranberries in a large bowl; stir well to combine. Squeeze as much liquid out of the cranberries as you can. You can put then in a fine strainer and push the liquid out with your hands. When they are as dry as possible, fold cranberries into the batter and spoon the batter into prepared muffin cups. You will get 5 to 6 muffins. Place in oven and bake for 20 to 25 minutes. Allow to cool. Muffins taste best the day they are baked, but they can be frozen for up to 3 months.

CORN MUFFINS

██

This is a delicious corn muffin, denser and grainier than many. It is great for breakfast with raspberry jam, but this is a versatile recipe that can be made with sweet or savory flavors. Try baking it in an 8 x 8-inch square pan for your next ribs barbeque, perhaps folding in a few chopped jalapeños or substituting blue instead of yellow cornmeal.

MAKES 6 MUFFINS

¼ cup granulated sugar

¼ cup brown sugar

1 extra-large egg

½ cup melted unsalted butter

1 cup buttermilk

1 cup all-purpose flour

1¼ cups fine yellow cornmeal

1 tsp. baking soda

½ tsp. salt

Preheat oven to 350°F. Spray a 12-muffin (½-cup capacity) pan. Combine all ingredients in a large bowl and mix well. Fill 6 muffin cups completely. Place in oven and bake for 20 to 25 minutes. These muffins will be done when firm to the touch, not browned completely. Allow to cool. Muffins taste best the day they are baked, but can be frozen for up to 3 months.

BRAN MUFFINS

▰▰

Almost all my muffin recipes evolved when I was at Fraser Morris experimenting with my talented coworker Sandy Cooper. One day she brought in a version of this recipe and we both liked the idea of whole wheat flour and pure wheat bran flakes. We decided to use currants instead of raisins because they were a staple ingredient in our rugelach. People often ask me which muffin is the least fattening. Perhaps it's this one—it's certainly the most nutritious and contains the highest amount of fiber (if anyone cares).

MAKES 4–6 MUFFINS

1 extra-large egg	1 cup whole wheat flour
¼ cup unsalted butter, melted	1¼ cups Millers bran*
¼ cup molasses	1 tsp. baking soda
¾ cup buttermilk	¼ tsp. salt
¼ cup water	½ tsp. cinnamon
¼ cup brown sugar	¼ cup currants

Preheat oven to 350°F. Spray a 12-muffin (½-cup capacity) pan. Combine all ingredients in a large bowl and stir well to combine. Spoon batter into the muffin cups, filling to the top. For a larger muffin, you can mound the batter up. You will get 4 to 6 muffins. Place in the oven and bake for 15 to 20 minutes or until centers are firm and tops are lightly browned. Allow to cool completely. Muffins taste best the day they are baked, but they can be wrapped in plastic and kept in the freezer for up to 3 months.

---

* Millers bran or unprocessed wheat bran is available in most health food stores.

RUGELACH

I am most proud of my rugelach recipe. At Fraser Morris we rolled hundreds of pounds of rugelach. In the basement in Brooklyn, we rolled hundreds of pounds of rugelach. At our house, the freezer was filled to capacity with rugelach. The table is worn down by all the cuts we make with rugelach. I see my daughter Julie eating raw rugelach dough as a baby and sister Katie throwing currants on the floor from the filling, my father eating scraps left on the pan. In 1997, I won WNYC public radio's best rugelach contest and everyone in my kitchen cheered. And oh, the compliments!

MAKES 48 PIECES

Dough:
1¼ pounds unsalted butter at room
    temperature
12 oz. cream cheese
¾ cup confectioners' sugar
3 cups all-purpose flour

Filling:
½–¾ cup apricot jam
1 cup ground walnuts
1 cup granulated sugar
½ cup currants
1 tbsp. cinnamon

Make the dough:
Beat butter until smooth in bowl of electric mixer, add cream cheese, and beat until well combined. Add confectioners' sugar, and then slowly add flour until completely incorporated. Place dough in a bowl, cover with plastic wrap, and refrigerate for at least 2 hours or overnight.

Remove dough from refrigerator and divide into 3 equal pieces. Put flour in a small bowl to use while rolling the rugelach. Work each piece of rugelach dough on a floured surface to form 3 smooth balls. Tear off three square pieces of wax paper to roll dough on. Be sure there is no flour under the surface of the wax paper. Place paper down and flour it heavily. Place a piece of dough on top of the floured paper and press it down with the palm of your hand to flatten slightly. Put

Continued on next page

more flour on top of dough. With a long-tapered rolling pin, begin to roll dough until you have a smooth circle 12 inches in diameter. Pick the circle up with wax paper still attached and place on a cookie sheet that will fit in your refrigerator. Repeat with other two pieces of dough, carefully layering one on top of the other. Make sure there is a little flour on the surface of each circle. Put cookie sheet in refrigerator for at least 2 hours. Well-chilled circles are essential.

Make the filling:
Preheat oven to 350°F. Line a 10 x 15-inch cookie sheet with parchment. To roll rugelach, you need the rugelach dough and filling ingredients listed above as well as a bench scraper, a cup measure, a small, sharp knife, and

an offset spatula. Work with one circle of dough at a time. Put circle on table without paper and dust off excess flour. Spread 2 to 3 tablespoons of apricot jam on the surface of circle, spreading almost to edge. Combine all other filling ingredients in a bowl. Put one cup of filling on the circle and spread it almost to the edge. With a small, sharp knife, cut the circle into 16 pie-shaped pieces. Starting with the outside edge, roll each pie-shaped piece all the way to the middle and place on parchment–lined cookie sheet. Repeat with other two circles. Bake rugelach for 20 to 25 minutes or until lightly browned. Allow to cool.

Rugelach keeps for up to 1 week in an airtight container.

DECORATED COOKIES

Whenever I think about decorated cookies, Patti Paige comes to mind—artist, baker, and owner of Baked Ideas, a custom bakery in NYC. Patti has raised the decorated cookie to an art form. I'm lucky to have hired some talented cookie decorators: decorator and musician Geoff Mann decorated a piano cookie with all twenty-six keys, Faina added bows to the socks of my little girl cookies, and thanks to Paul's smart merchandizing the cookies are in a display case at a child's eye level! Decorated cookies give kids much pleasure and keep me inventing new ones.

MAKES 36–48 (2-INCH) COOKIES OR 24 (3-INCH) LINZER TART COOKIES

Sugar cookie dough:

1 cup unsalted butter at room temperature

1 cup granulated sugar

2 extra-large eggs

1 tbsp. pure vanilla extract

3 cup all-purpose flour

½ tsp. baking soda

½ tsp. salt

Royal icing:

½ cup egg whites (whites from approximately 8 eggs)

5½ cups confectioners' sugar

Make the dough:

In the bowl of an electric mixer, beat the butter and sugar until well combined. Break the eggs into a small bowl and then add them to the mixer bowl with the vanilla. Beat until all ingredients are incorporated. Measure flour, baking soda, and salt into a bowl and slowly add them to the mixer, beating on low speed until the flour is combined. Turn dough out onto surface, wrap with plastic wrap, and place in the refrigerator for at least 2 hours or overnight. This is enough dough to make at least 36 to 48 (2-inch) cookies, or 24 (3-inch) linzer tart cookies. You can keep the dough in the refrigerator for up to 1 week or freeze for up to 3 months.

Line your cookie sheet with parchment paper or spray. When dough is well chilled, cut the piece of dough in half. Put one half on a lightly floured surface and put the other back in the refrigerator. Only roll one small piece of dough at a time. With a bench scraper, cut the dough into a few pieces and then gather them together. Work them on the surface until the dough becomes a smooth ball. Place the ball on the floured work surface and press it down slightly. Flour the top of the dough and with a traditional rolling pin start rolling away from yourself. Turn the dough a little and repeat. It is best to continue to roll in one direction, not back-and-forth. Keep turning the dough as you go, making sure you have flour underneath the dough. Without sufficient flour, it will be hard to move the dough. If you discover no flour under your dough, sprinkle the edges around the dough with flour and run a

Continued on next page

string under the dough. (See photo.) Continue to roll the dough until it is about ¼-inch thick all around. Cut out the dough with any cutter you like, starting at the edge of the dough and working toward the center. You can lift the cookies off the table with your hands but if you have trouble use an offset spatula dipped into flour. Place the cookies next to each other on the cookie sheet but not touching. Pull together the extra dough, cover in plastic wrap, and refrigerate. Repeat this procedure with the rest of the dough. Place the cookies in the oven and bake for 10 to 12 minutes. They should be lightly brown; do not over bake. Allow to cool completely.

Make the icing:

There are many ways to decorate a cookie. This way works best for me. You will need a lot of equipment (refer to pg. 5). You must have more than one pastry bag, food colors, offset spatula, patience, determination, and a steady hand. Place the egg whites in the bowl of an electric mixer with the whisk attachment and beat until stiff peaks form. Change to the paddle attachment and slowly add the confectioners' sugar. Beat on slow speed until all the sugar is added. If the confectioners' sugar is lumpy put it through a sifter or strainer before adding to the egg whites. Beat the mixture well until all sugar is added. It should be as thick as whipped cream cheese. It is important to place the royal icing in a plastic container with a tight lid. Air makes royal icing dry out and crunchy spots can form.

Decorate the cookies:

There are plain cookies with decorations, there are dipped cookies with decorations, and there are combinations of the two. Most of the decorated cookies I make are dipped first. Then I pipe decorations on top of the dried icing. I use colored sugar (sometimes called sanding sugar) for many of the cookies and they are available in many specialty markets and online. Regular granulated sugar does not work. The best way to get good at cookie decorating is practice. I recommend doing ten identical cookies. By the tenth cookie you will be an expert! Then move to a new shape. The pastry bag can get clogged and then the icing will stop flowing. When this happens, run the tip under very hot water while you continue to squeeze the bag. Usually this will dissolve the clog. Sometimes you need to remove the tip and wash it. You can keep the bags for a couple of days, store them in a re-sealable bag or a plastic container with a tight lid.

Dipping:

For dipping cookies, the consistency of royal icing has to be like latex paint—thick but spreadable. Use a round layer pan or a shallow soup bowl for dipping. Fill the bowl to about two inches from the top. (Make sure to cover the container of icing after each use.) Have water in a cup or squirt bottle nearby. If you want to

make a white-dipped cookie, you only need to add a few drops of water to give the icing the correct consistency. A too-thin consistency and the cookie will show through, and too thick will not be smooth enough. If you want to dip cookies in other colors, put a few drops of food coloring into the icing and stir. Then add the water drop by drop. You can make as many colors are you want at the same time. Remember to cover the bowl tightly with plastic wrap until needed. To dip a cookie, pick it up with your left hand (if you are right handed) holding the cookie by the sides. Hold the offset spatula in your dominant hand. Dip the cookie into the prepared icing, lift it up, let excess icing fall back into the bowl, swipe your spatula down, and scrape off excess from the bottom of the cookie. Place the cookie down on the cookie sheet and repeat until all are dipped. When you are completely finished dipping, place each colored icing in its own plastic container with an airtight lid. You can use the colors again. You may need to add water to get to the proper consistency. Icing will only last two or three days—even in an airtight container.

Piping:

After all the cookies are dipped they need several hours to dry before you can pipe on them. It is best to give them a day to dry. For piping decorations on the cookies, you will need a lot of equipment (refer to pg. 5). You will need 12-inch pastry bags, couplers, tips, and icing of a slightly different consistency. The icing should be stiff for writing and making thin lines or looser for filling in and making outlines. Assemble your 12-inch pastry bag with a coupler and tip and set aside. Put ¾ cup of icing in a small bowl. Add a few drops of color to the icing and then a few drops of water. Make sure you incorporate the color and stir the icing so there are no lumps. The icing should be the consistency of soft peanut butter. If it is too thin you can add more confectioners' sugar. The best way to fill the pastry bag is to put it into a firm plastic cup, roll the edge of the bag around the outside of the cup, and guide the icing into the bag with a rubber spatula. Twist the edges of the pastry bag together so the icing does not come out of the top. It's a good idea to practice by piping on a cookie sheet or any flat surface before piping on the cookie. Start with an easy line or the center of a flower cookie. To use sanding sugar (sparkly colored sugar), pour some sugar on a piece of wax paper. Pipe a big dot of icing such as the center of a daisy shaped cookie. Lift the cookie up and turn it over into the sanding. The sugar will stick to the dot of icing and make it sparkle. It's fun to get creative with the sugar accents. We always make Santa's beard sparkle!

OATMEAL RAISIN COOKIES

The oatmeal raisin cookie is next in popularity after the chocolate chip cookie. I have tried using dried cranberries, chocolate chips, nuts, once even Froot Loops! I've tried oat bran when it was trendy and made a gluten-free version (nobody is immune to the latest food fads), but I always come back to the traditional oatmeal raisin cookie—this recipe has staying power.

MAKES 36 COOKIES

1½ cups unsalted butter at room
    temperature
1 cup granulated sugar
2 cups brown sugar
2 extra-large eggs
½ tsp. vanilla
¼ cup water

2 cups all-purpose flour
3 cups quick oats
¾ tsp. baking soda
¼ tsp. salt
¼ tsp. cinnamon
2 cups raisins

Preheat oven to 350°F. Spray a 10 x 15-inch cookie sheet or line with parchment. In the bowl of an electric mixer beat the butter and sugars until well combined. Break eggs in a small bowl and add to the mixer with the vanilla and water. Beat until combined. Measure flour, oats, baking soda, salt, and cinnamon into a bowl and add to mixer. Beat on low speed until combined, then add the raisins. Form the dough into balls about the size of a ping pong ball on the cookie sheet. If the dough is very soft you can chill it for about 30 minutes so it will be easier to form into balls. The cookies will spread while baking, so fit no more than 8 to a cookie sheet. Bake for 10 to 12 minutes or until lightly brown. Allow to cool completely. Make more cookies or store dough in the refrigerator for up to 2 weeks or frozen for up to 3 months.

PECAN BALLS

This is a Christmas cookie. Of course, you can make it anytime, but traditionally it belongs on your Christmas cookie platter. You can use other nuts, but pecans are my favorite. My first customer for them every year is Kathy Burke—she can smell them baking from up the street! I guarantee you'll be asked to make them every year.

MAKES 30–36 PECAN BALLS

1 cup unsalted butter at room temperature
¼ cup granulated sugar
¾ tsp. vanilla

2 cups all-purpose flour
2 cups pecans, finely chopped
1 cup confectioners' sugar

Preheat oven to 350°F. Spray a 10 x 15-inch cookie sheet or line with parchment. Cream butter and sugar in the bowl of an electric mixer, add vanilla, and mix until incorporated. Add flour and pecans and beat on low speed until thoroughly combined. Form cookies into walnut-size balls and place them on cookie sheet, near each other but not touching. Place in oven and bake for 12 to 15 minutes or until very lightly brown. Allow to cool. Place confectioners' sugar in a bowl and roll cookies in sugar, coating them thoroughly. You have made beautiful little snowballs. Use all dough at one time or wrap in plastic wrap and refrigerate for up to 2 weeks or freeze for up to 3 months.

CARROT CAKE

▪▪

We made carrot cake every day at Fraser Morris. When we put out a large carrot Bundt cake in the morning and it was gone by lunchtime, we knew we had a great recipe. I continued to do this when we moved to Brooklyn. One year someone asked me to share a table at the Atlantic Antic, the largest street fair in Brooklyn. I agreed but wasn't sure what to sell that would be easy to transport. I decided to bake the carrot cake in a full sheet pan, frosting the top, and cutting it into squares. It was one of the best decisions I ever made. By the time I retire I will have sold close to a million carrot cake squares!

MAKES 1 (10-INCH) CAKE, 25 SERVINGS OR 15 (3-INCH) SQUARES

Cake:

6 carrots, grated in the food processor

2 cups granulated sugar

1½ cups melted butter

1 cup chopped walnuts

4 extra-large eggs

2 cups all-purpose flour

½ tsp. cinnamon

2¼ tsp. baking soda

¼ tsp. salt

Cream cheese frosting:

½ cup unsalted butter at room temperature

8 oz. cream cheese at room temperature

1 tsp. pure vanilla extract

3 cups confectioners' sugar

Make cake:

Preheat oven to 350°F. Spray and line with parchment a 10 x 15 x 3-inch cake pan, or spray and line 2 (10-inch) layer pans with parchment paper. Place grated carrots, sugar, melted butter, walnuts, and eggs in the bowl of an electric mixer. Beat until ingredients are combined. Measure flour, cinnamon, baking soda, and salt in a bowl, add it to the mixer bowl, and beat until well mixed. Pour into prepared pan or pans and bake 35 to 45 minutes or until the middle of the cake is firm to the touch and the cake is pulling away from the sides of the pan. Allow to cool completely. It is easier to ice the cake if you freeze it first for 30 minutes.

Make frosting:

In the bowl of an electric mixer, cream butter and add the cream cheese. Beat until well combined and completely smooth and scrape down the bowl often so no lumps stick to the sides. Add vanilla and confectioners' sugar, (if the confectioners' sugar is lumpy, strain it through a sieve

Continued on next page

before adding to the butter and cream cheese mixture). Beat on low speed until sugar in incorporated, then increase speed and beat until light and fluffy, about 5 minutes.

For the single layer rectangle, spread icing on top of cake in one smooth layer, leaving it in the pan. Chill cake and cut into squares. For the layer cake, remove cakes from their pans, peel paper from the bottom of one layer and place it on a flat plate. Carrot cake does not usually rise, but if the top is not flat, take a long serrated knife and level the cake by placing the knife horizontally against the side of the cake and turn the cake as you cut. Do the same thing with the other layer. You are only taking off a small amount of cake. Frost bottom layer with ½ inch of frosting. Place the second layer on top of the first one and place the cake in the freezer to harden for about 1 hour.

Frost the cake:

The best way to frost a cake is on a cake stand that is also a turntable. If you plan to make layer cakes, this is a necessary piece of equipment to own. When the cake is very firm, place on the turntable and frost the sides of the cake with an offset spatula. Smooth the frosting around the sides of the cake in a layer thick enough so that none of the cake is visible. When the sides are completely covered, place some frosting on the top. Spread frosting to make an even layer on the top of the cake. You can make a frosting border around the edge of the cake or press chopped walnuts into the side of the cake. (Use the same technique described for putting crumbs on the Blackout Chocolate Cake on pg. 113.) This is a very moist cake; it will keep for up to 5 days.

PECAN PIE

When Thanksgiving rolls around everyone is looking for a pie. Pecan pie is always great because it's not fragile, has a long shelf life, and you usually only eat it once in a while so you can really indulge when you do and have it with a big scoop of vanilla ice cream.

MAKES 10–12 SERVINGS

Pâte brisée (pie dough):
3 cups all-purpose flour
2 tbsp. granulated sugar
¼ tsp. salt
½ cup unsalted butter, well chilled
½ cup vegetable shortening, well chilled
½ cup ice water
2 bags dried beans* any variety

Filling:
1½ cups pecan halves
6 extra-large eggs
2 cups dark corn syrup
1 cup granulated sugar
4 tbsp. unsalted melted butter
2 tsp. vanilla

Make pâte brisée (pie dough):

Put the flour, sugar, and salt in the bowl of a food processor with metal blade. Cut butter into small pieces and add it to bowl along with shortening. Pulse the mixture until butter and shortening is completely combined with the flour. With food processor running, slowly pour in ice water. The mixture should just come together—you don't want it to be sticky. Crumbly is fine. Turn dough out on a floured surface and pull the dough together with your hands to form a ball. If it seems too dry, sprinkle a few drops of water directly on the dough. Wrap the dough in plastic wrap and refrigerate for at least 2 hours.

Remove dough from the refrigerator and cut off about a quarter of the dough (or weighing .47 on a food scale, if you have one). Use a long, thin, tapered rolling pin. Put your rolling pin down in the middle of the dough and start rolling away from you. Turn the dough slightly in a clockwise direction and roll again. Keep doing this until you have a circle about 10 inches in diameter. Place it in a 9-inch

Continued on next page

---

* I must give credit for this method of "blind baking" to Emily Isaac. She worked with us when Zucker's shared the space. She is a talented baker and a lovely person. Thank you, Emily—this method is really great!

pie plate and make a decorative edge. Freeze pie plate for about 30 minutes and then line bottom of pie with a double layer of plastic wrap, placing one large piece in one direction and other piece in the other direction. Then fill it with dried beans (also known as pie weights) and bring plastic wrap up around the beans. (See photo.) It should completely fill the pie plate, even rise up over the top a little. What you're doing is called "blind baking" and ensures that the pie crust will be thoroughly baked. Preheat oven to 350°F. Place pie shell in the oven and bake for 35 to 40 minutes or until the edges of the pie are lightly brown. Remove from oven and allow to cool completely. Remove the beans and save them for your next pie.

Make filling:
Preheat oven to 350°F. To fill the pie shell, scatter the pecan halves. In a large bowl, beat the eggs, corn syrup, sugar, butter, and vanilla. Stir with a whisk until no egg is visible. Pour over pecan halves. Place pie in the oven and bake for 35 to 40 minutes or until the edges of the pie are lightly brown. Remove from oven and allow to cool completely. The pie will keep up to 1 week in the refrigerator.

PECAN TARTS

I have always loved pecan pie, but it can taste too sweet after a few bites. These tarts are a perfect solution. The ratio of filling to pecans to crust is just right. They are also very easy to make. The pecan halves glisten on the top, and when served with a scoop of vanilla ice cream they are irresistible.

MAKES 1 (8-INCH) TART OR 3 (4-INCH) TARTS, 6–8 SERVINGS

Pâte brisée (tart dough):
3 cups all-purpose flour
2 tbsp. granulated sugar
¼ tsp. salt
1 cup unsalted butter, well chilled
½ cup ice water

Filling:
1 cup pecan halves
3 extra-large eggs
1 cup dark corn syrup
½ cup granulated sugar
2 tbsp. unsalted melted butter
1 tsp. vanilla

Make pâte brisée (tart dough):
Put the flour, sugar, and salt in the bowl of a food processor with metal blade. Cut butter into small pieces and add it to bowl. Pulse the mixture until butter is completely combined with the flour. With food processor running, slowly pour in ice water. The mixture should just come together—you don't want it to be sticky. Crumbly is fine. Turn dough out on a floured surface and pull the dough together with your hands to form a ball. If it seems too dry, sprinkle a few drops of water directly on the dough. Wrap the dough in plastic wrap and refrigerate for at least 2 hours. Take the dough out of the refrigerator and divide it into 4 pieces. Each piece will fill an 8-inch tart shell. For 4-inch tarts, divide one of the quarters into three. (Freeze or refrigerate other pieces of dough for another time.) Flour the work surface. Form the dough into a ball with your hands. Place the ball of dough on the floured work surface and press it down. Lightly flour the top of the dough. Use a long, thin, tapered rolling pin. Put your rolling pin down in the middle of the dough and start rolling away from you. Turn the dough slightly in a clockwise direction and roll again. Keep doing this until you have a circle about 10 inches in diameter. Place the dough on top of the tart shell. Please refer to photo on pg. 47 to guide you in placing dough into the shell. With the heel of your hand remove the excess dough. The tart shell is now ready to fill.

Make filling:
Preheat oven to 350 °F. Scatter the pecan halves on the tart shell or shells. In a large bowl beat the eggs, corn syrup, sugar, butter, and vanilla. Stir with a whisk until no egg is visible. Pour over pecan halves in each tart shell. Carefully place the tart shells in the oven and bake for 30 to 35 minutes or until the filling is completely set. Allow to cool.

PASSOVER CHOCOLATE NUT TORTE

■■

This recipe belongs to the family of my boss from Fraser Morris. Blossom Bromberg gave me this very good torte recipe to make for Passover. I have loyal customers who order this torte every year. The apples keep the cake moist, and the walnuts and chocolate mask the taste of the matzo meal, so get ready to add this to your Passover menu—it will be a hit.

MAKES 12–14 SERVINGS

6 extra-large eggs, separated

1½ cups granulated sugar

1 cup walnuts, finely chopped

¾ cups semi-sweet chocolate chips

2 Granny Smith apples, peeled, cored, chopped in the food processor

10 tbsp. matzo meal

Preheat oven to 350°F. Spray 1 (8-inch) layer pan and line with parchment. Put egg yolks and sugar in the bowl of an electric mixer and beat until light for 5 minutes. Add walnuts, chocolate chips, apples, and matzo meal. Beat to combine all ingredients. Move mixture to a clean mixer bowl. With whisk, beat egg whites in a separate bowl until soft peaks are formed. Fold into batter gently—do not deflate whites. Pour batter into prepared pan and bake for 40 to 45 minutes or until firm to the touch. Keeps for 4 days well wrapped.

MIXED BERRY TARTS

▪▪▪

The French are the prime source of inspiration when it comes to tarts. A filling recipe for cooked fruit tarts appears in every French cookbook. It is traditionally made with hazelnuts, but I have always used toasted almonds. I make large batches of it once a week and use it to fill not only the mixed berry tarts, but cherry tarts, peach tarts, plum tarts, or almost any fruit that is seasonal and available.

MAKES 6–8 SLICES

Pâte brisée (tart dough):
3 cups all-purpose flour
2 tbsp. granulated sugar
¼ tsp. salt
1 cup unsalted butter, well
    chilled
½ cup ice water
1 (8-inch) fluted tart shell
    filled with pastry,
    unbaked

Tart filling:
2 cups sliced almonds
1 cup unsalted butter at
    room temperature
1⅔ cups confectioners'
    sugar
3 extra-large eggs
1 cup fresh or frozen
    blueberries
1 cup fresh or frozen
    raspberries

Glaze:
1 cup apricot jam

Make pâte brisée (tart dough):
Put the flour, sugar, and salt in the bowl of a food processor with metal blade. Cut the butter into small pieces and add it to the bowl. Pulse the mixture until the butter is completely combined with the flour. With the food processor running, slowly pour in the ice water. The mixture should just come together—you don't want it to be sticky. Crumbly is fine. Turn dough out on a floured surface and pull the dough together with your hands to form a ball. If it seems too dry, sprinkle a few drops of water directly on the dough. Wrap the dough in plastic wrap and refrigerate for at least 2 hours. Take the dough out of the refrigerator and divide it into 4 pieces. Each piece will fill an 8-inch tart shell. (Freeze or refrigerate other pieces of dough for another time.) Flour the work surface. Form the dough into a ball with your hands. Place the ball of dough on the floured work surface and press it down. Lightly

flour the top of the dough. Use a long, thin, tapered rolling pin. Put your rolling pin down in the middle of the dough and start rolling away from you. Turn the dough slightly in a clockwise direction and roll again. Keep doing this until you have a circle about 10 inches in diameter. Place the dough on top of the tart shell. Please refer to photo to guide you in placing dough into the shell. With the heel of your hand remove the excess dough. It is now ready to fill.

Make filling:
Preheat oven to 350°F. Put sliced almonds on a cookie sheet and put in the oven to toast. After 5 minutes toss the almonds with a spoon so they will brown evenly. Toast for another 5 minutes. Allow to cool completely. Place almonds in the bowl of a food processor with metal blade and grind finely. Beat butter and confectioners' sugar in the bowl of the electric mixer until well combined. Break eggs in a cup and add to the mixer; beat well. Then add the almonds and mix until all ingredients are well combined. Spread 3/4-inch layer of the filling on an 8-inch fluted tart shell which you have filled with pastry. Spread blueberries on top, and then raspberries. It will seem like a lot of fruit but it will bake down. Bake the tart for 45 to 50 minutes until the edges brown and the middle sets. Allow to cool.

Make glaze:
Put apricot jam in a small saucepan. Place over medium heat and stir until jam becomes liquified. You want to use the liquid, not the fruit, for the glaze. Remove tart from outer ring of tart shell. Place tart on serving plate with its metal bottom (a way to prevent disasters). With a pastry brush, carefully but generously apply the apricot jam to the top of the tart. Let cool. This tart will stay fresh in the refrigerator for up to 4 days.

APPLE PIE

▰▰▰

Patsy Blackman, my second employee, always comes to my mind when I think about apple pie. Nobody has ever piled the apples up so beautifully, made as perfect an edge, brushed the egg wash, and sprinkled the sugar as well as Patsy! Her attention to detail was an important lesson for me. Professional bakers often look for shortcuts because they have so much to do. Patsy didn't believe in shortcuts.

MAKES 6–8 SLICES

Pie dough:

1 (9-inch) pie plate (preferably Pyrex)

3 cups all-purpose flour

2 tbsp. granulated sugar

¼ tsp. salt

½ cup unsalted butter, well chilled

½ cup vegetable shortening, well chilled

½ cup ice water

Filling:

5–7 apples*, assorted varieties, at least 2 Granny Smiths

½ cup granulated sugar

1 tsp. cinnamon

¼ tsp. salt

2 tbsp. all-purpose flour

2 tbsp. unsalted butter

2 eggs, beaten, for egg wash to brush on top of crust

2 tbsp. raw sugar for sprinkling on the top of the pie

Make dough:

Put the flour, sugar, and salt in the bowl of a food processor with metal blade. Cut the butter and vegetable shortening into small pieces and add it to the bowl. Pulse the mixture until the butter is completely combined with the flour. With food processor running, slowly pour in ice water. The mixture should just come together—you don't want it to be sticky. Crumbly is fine. Turn dough out on a floured surface and pull the dough together with your hands to form a ball. If it seems too dry, sprinkle a few drops of water directly on the dough. Wrap the dough in plastic wrap and refrigerate for at least 2 hours. Take the dough out of the refrigerator, divide it into 2 pieces. Return 1 piece to the refrigerator. Form each piece of dough into a ball and place on a floured work surface, pressing it down. Lightly flour the top of the dough. Put a long, thin, tapered rolling pin down in the middle of the dough and start rolling away from you. Turn the dough slightly in a

Continued on next page

---

* It is important to use a variety of apples in this recipe, don't cut the apples into very small pieces, and always pile the filling higher than you think reasonable.

clockwise direction and roll again. Make sure there is always flour under the dough. Keep rolling until you have a circle about 10 inches in diameter. Place the dough on top of the pie plate. It is now ready to fill.

Make filling:
Preheat oven to 350°F. Peel, core, and cut apples and place in a large bowl. Add rest of the ingredients to the bowl except butter, eggs, and raw sugar. Toss the ingredients with the apples and let sit for 15 minutes or until juices are released. Pile apples into pie shell, cut butter into small pieces, and place on top of apples. Roll top crust as indicated above and drape gently on top of the apples. Center dough to hang equally all around. Press the edges together on rim of pie plate and roll the edges up all around. Crimp edges to form a decorative border (see photo). Place pie on a cookie sheet and brush top of pie liberally with egg wash. Be sure not to leave any spots unbrushed. Score the top with a sharp knife—this allows steam and juices to be released. I make the cuts into a star pattern. Sprinkle the top with raw sugar and place in the oven for 1 hour or 1 hour and 10 minutes. The top should be beautifully browned and juices should be coming out of the air holes. If baked in a Pyrex pie plate, lift the pie to see if the bottom is brown. Allow to cool.

PUMPKIN PIE

My brother Joe Palca comes to mind when I make pumpkin pie. He always loved Horn and Hardart's pumpkin pie. Perhaps its attraction was that store-bought baked goods were rare in our house. The pie came in a window box and had a shiny top. I believe all pumpkin pies should have a shiny top. It has taken me a while to master the look I feel is important. I have made many versions over the years, but this recipe is the best. Putting shelled pumpkin seeds around the outside edge is my contribution. What a nice way to unite the different parts of the pumpkin.

MAKES 8–10 SERVINGS

Pie crust:
3 cups all-purpose flour
2 tbsp. granulated sugar
¼ tsp. salt
½ cup unsalted butter, well chilled
½ cup vegetable shortening, well chilled
½ cup ice water
2 (1-pound) bags dried beans*

Filling:
¾ cup granulated sugar
⅓ cup brown sugar
¼ tsp. salt
1 tsp. cinnamon
½ tsp. ginger
¼ tsp. allspice
2 extra-large eggs
2 cups pumpkin purée
1⅓ cups milk
1 cup evaporated milk
¼ cup pumpkin seeds

Make crust:
Put the flour, sugar, and salt in bowl of a food processor with metal blade. Cut butter and shortening into small pieces and add it to bowl. Pulse mixture until the butter is completely combined with flour. With food processor running, slowly pour in ice water. The mixture should just come together—you don't want it to be sticky. Crumbly is fine. Turn dough out on floured surface and pull dough together with your hands to form ball. If it seems dry, sprinkle a few drops of water directly on dough. Wrap dough in plastic wrap and refrigerate for at least 2 hours. Remove dough from the refrigerator and cut off about

Continued on next page

---

* I give credit for this method of "blind baking" to Emily Isaac. She worked with me when Zucker's shared my space. A talented baker and a lovely person. Thank you, Emily, for sharing your knowledge.

a quarter of the dough (or weighing .47 on a food scale, if you have one). Return other pieces to refrigerator or freezer for another pie. Flour work surface. Form dough into a ball with your hands. Place ball of dough on floured work surface and press it down. Lightly flour top of the dough. Use a long, thin, tapered rolling pin. Put rolling pin in the middle of dough and start rolling away from you. Turn dough a little at a time in a clockwise direction and roll again until you have a circle about 10 inches in diameter. Place dough in 9-inch pie plate and make a decorative edge. Freeze the pie plate for 30 minutes.

Preheat oven to 350°F. Line bottom of pie plate with a double layer of plastic wrap, placing one large piece in one direction and another piece in the other direction. Fill with dried beans and bring plastic wrap up around beans. They should completely fill the pie plate. What you're doing is called "blind baking" and ensures that the pie crust will be thoroughly baked. Place pie shell in oven and bake for 35 to 40 minutes or until edges of shell are lightly brown. Remove from oven and allow to cool completely. Remove beans and save them for your next pie.

Make filling:
Put granulated sugar, brown sugar, salt, cinnamon, ginger, and all-spice in a large bowl and mix with whisk. Add eggs and pumpkin purée and mix well. Carefully stir in milks. Pour mixture into prepared pie shell—it will be very full. Carefully place on oven rack. Bake for 35 to 45 minutes. The top will be slightly wet in middle when done—better to err on the side of underdone. When cool, sprinkle outside edge of pie with pumpkin seeds. Pie keeps in the refrigerator for 3 to 4 days and freezes for up to 3 months.

CHAPTER FOUR

THE BASEMENT IN BROOKLYN

SOUR CREAM COFFEE CAKE

▪▪

I've been making this delicious cake for a very long time. I don't remember exactly where the recipe came from, but baked in a Bundt pan and sprinkled with confectioners' sugar, this beautiful cake is a staple on the counter of my cafe.

MAKES 12–14 SERVINGS

Cake:
1 cup unsalted butter at room temperature
¾ cup granulated sugar
2 extra-large eggs
1 cup sour cream
1½ cups all-purpose flour
1 tsp. pure vanilla extract
1½ tsp. baking powder
1 tsp. baking soda
¼ tsp. salt

Filling:
⅓ cup granulated sugar
⅓ cup brown sugar
1 tsp. cinnamon
½ cup currants
½ cup chopped walnuts

Make cake:
Preheat oven to 350°F. Spray a 10-inch Bundt pan. Place butter and sugar in the bowl of an electric mixer and beat on medium speed until light and fluffy. Break eggs into a small bowl and add eggs to sugar mixture. Add sour cream to mixer bowl and beat. Measure flour, vanilla, baking powder, baking soda, and salt in a bowl; add slowly. Gradually increase speed and mix until combined but do not overbeat. Scrape down the bowl with a rubber spatula.

Make filling:
Combine filling ingredients in a bowl. Place half of cake batter in prepared pan and sprinkle with half filling. Then cover with rest of batter and sprinkle top with remaining filling. With a knife, swirl the filling throughout the cake. None of the filling should be visible on top of cake. Place in oven and bake for 50 to 60 minutes until a thin long knife inserted comes out clean. The cake should be brown on top and firm to the touch. Allow to cool completely before unmolding. You may need to run a knife around the edge of the pan and gently tap the sides of the pan to help release the cake. Place a plate on top of the cake and then turn it over. Sprinkle with confectioners' sugar. Cake keeps for 4 days well wrapped.

APPLE LOAF CAKE

This is one of the first loaf cakes I ever made. I started out putting the apples on top of the cake, but that made the cake sink in the middle! Now I make a thin layer of cake followed by a layer of sliced apples tossed with cinnamon and sugar and then another layer of cake. This layering results in a very moist cake. You can serve this apple cake at your next brunch or tea party.

MAKES 10–12 SLICES

1 Granny Smith apple
3 tbsp. granulated sugar + 2 cups
½ tsp. cinnamon
2⅔ cups all-purpose flour
1 tbsp. baking powder

½ tsp. salt
4 extra-large eggs
1 cup canola oil
⅓ cup orange juice

Preheat oven to 350°F. Spray a 10-inch Bundt pan or a 9 x 9-inch loaf pan. Peel, core, and slice the apple into a bowl and toss with 3 tbsp. sugar and cinnamon. Measure flour, baking powder, and salt into a separate bowl. Break eggs in another bowl and then add to the bowl of the electric mixer. Beat on medium speed, then add the remaining sugar and beat until eggs have lightened in color, about 5 minutes. Reduce speed and add the canola oil and orange juice. Slowly add in the flour mixture and beat until all ingredients are well combined. Pour half the batter in the bottom of the prepared pan and place a layer of apples on top of the batter. Cover the apples with the rest of the batter. If you are making a loaf, decorate the top with a few slices of apple before placing in the oven. Bake for 50 to 55 minutes or until a cake tester or thin long knife comes out clean. Allow to cool completely. This cake lasts about 1 week well wrapped.

YELLOW CAKE

▰▰

In 1985, we moved into a small house on Carroll Street in Brooklyn. The garden level of the house was one large room—perfect for setting up a professional kitchen. We installed ovens, refrigerators, work tables, and storage shelves. I soon realized I needed help, put an ad in the paper, and hired my first employee, Marcia Bishop. This recipe for yellow cake was a gift from her. She was a great cake baker, always making cakes for her fellow churchgoers. We worked together for many years, and I learned a great deal from her—every time I make a yellow cake I think of Marcia by my side. In 2020, Marcia contracted the coronavirus and passed away. Fortunately, her memory will always live on in me and all the other lucky people who knew her and learned from her.

MAKES 25 SERVINGS

Cake:
2 cups unsalted butter at room
    temperature
2 cups granulated sugar
8 extra-large eggs
1 tsp. vanilla
2½ cups all-purpose flour
2½ tsp. baking powder

Vanilla buttercream:
1 cup unsalted butter at room temperature
½ tsp. pure vanilla extract
2 tbsp. heavy cream
3 cups confectioners' sugar

Make cake:
Preheat oven to 350°F. Spray 2 (10-inch) cake pans and line with parchment rounds. In the bowl of an electric mixer beat the butter and sugar until light and fluffy, about 10 minutes. It's important to beat the butter and sugar for a long time with this cake. Break the eggs into a bowl and add them to the machine, beating slowly. Then add vanilla. Measure the flour and baking powder into a small bowl and add to the mixer; beat until all the flour is combined. Do not overbeat. Place half of batter into each prepared pan and bake for 25 to 35 minutes or until the cake is lightly brown, firm in the center, and pulling away from the sides of the pan. Allow to cool completely.

Make buttercream:
In the bowl of an electric mixer beat butter, vanilla, and heavy cream until well combined. Slowly add the confectioners' sugar on low speed until all is added. Raise speed to high and beat until buttercream is a smooth and spreadable consistency.

Continued on next page

Assemble cake:

Place one cake layer on a flat serving plate and level the top with a long serrated knife by cutting the top of the layer, turning the cake slightly as you cut to make the top one even layer. Then cut the layer in half using the same method, but start in the middle of the layer and keep turning until you have cut all the way around. Do the same thing with the second cake. Separate all the layers; you should have one layer on your serving plate and the other three on your work surface.

Fill a 12-inch pastry bag with a coupler half-full with buttercream and on the first layer pipe a ring of buttercream around the edge of the cake. Place some buttercream inside the ring and smooth with an offset spatula to make one layer even with the ring. Repeat this process with the remaining layers. Place the final layer on top and freeze the cake for 45 minutes to 1 hour. Place the cake on a turntable. Place mixer bowl with buttercream on the left side of the turntable and remove paddle. With an offset spatula in your right hand, scoop some icing onto the spatula and place it on the sides of the cake. Smooth it out slightly and continue to do this all the way around the cake while turning the turntable with your left hand. As you cover each area, rotate the turntable. When all of the sides are iced, place your spatula on the side of the cake and spread and turn the cake until the icing is smooth all around. Then scoop some icing on the top of the cake, and with the offset spatula smooth it all around.

To pipe a border around the top and bottom edges of the cake, put a star tip on the pastry bag. You can also color some of the buttercream to pipe flowers and leaves as decoration or change the tip of the pastry bag to a writing tip and add an inscription on top of the cake. Serve cake at room temperature. It will keep for up to 5 days.

COCONUT LEMON CAKE

▞▚

Lemon curd is a wonderful filling for coconut cake. My mother says she always asked for a coconut lemon cake for her birthday when she was growing up. I don't have firsthand experience of this, but my mother assures me I make a pretty good version. Thanks, Mom.

MAKES 25 SERVINGS

Lemon curd:
3 extra-large eggs
   3 extra-large yolks
1½ cups granulated sugar
¼ tsp. salt
½ cup (3 or 4 lemons)
   lemon juice + lemon
   rinds, grated
½ cup unsalted butter

Cake:
2 cups unsalted butter at
   room temperature
2 cups granulated sugar
8 extra-large eggs
1 tsp. vanilla
2½ cups all-purpose flour
2½ tsp. baking powder
1½ cups sweetened flaked
   coconut, for topping

Vanilla buttercream:
1 cup unsalted butter at
   room temperature
½ tsp. pure vanilla extract
2 tbsp. heavy cream
3 cups confectioners'
   sugar

Make lemon curd:

Place separated eggs and yolks in a heavy bottomed stainless-steel saucepan. Add sugar and beat with a whisk to combine. Add salt, grated lemon rinds, and lemon juice and beat to combine. Add butter and place over medium to low heat. Whisk often while cooking. When the butter has completely melted, stir more often. Do not let the mixture come to a boil. It should be the thickness of a thin custard when done. Remove from heat and transfer to a bowl to cool. If you don't transfer the curd to a bowl, the heat from the pot will continue to cook it. When completely cool, store in a plastic container in the refrigerator. The lemon curd will keep at least 1 month.

Make cake:

Preheat oven to 350°F. Spray 2 (10-inch) cake pans and line with parchment rounds. In the bowl of an electric mixer beat the butter and sugar until light and fluffy, about 10 minutes. It's important to beat the butter and sugar for a long time with this cake. Break the eggs into a bowl and add them to the machine, beating slowly. Then add vanilla. Measure the flour and baking powder into a small bowl and add to the mixer; beat until all the flour is combined. Do not overbeat. Place half of batter into each prepared pan and bake for 25 to 35 minutes or until the cake is lightly brown, firm in the center, and pulling away from the sides of the pan. Allow to cool completely.

Continued on next page

Make buttercream:
In the bowl of an electric mixer beat butter, vanilla, and heavy cream until well combined. Slowly add the confectioners' sugar on low speed until all is added. Raise speed to high and beat until buttercream is a very smooth and spreadable consistency.

Assemble cake:
Place one cake layer on a flat serving plate and level the top with a long serrated knife by cutting the top of the layer, turning the cake slightly as you cut to make the top one even layer. Then cut the layer in half using the same method, but start in the middle of the layer and keep turning until you have cut all the way around. Do the same thing with the second cake. Separate all the layers; you should have one layer on your serving plate and the other three on your work surface.

Fill a 12-inch pastry bag with a coupler half-full with buttercream and on the first layer pipe a ring of buttercream around the edge of the cake. Spoon some lemon curd inside the ring and smooth it out with an offset spatula to make one layer within the ring. Repeat this process with the remaining layers. Place the final layer on top and freeze the cake for 45 minutes to 1 hour. Place the cake on a turntable. Place mixer bowl with buttercream on the left side of the turntable and remove paddle. With an offset spatula in your right hand, scoop some icing onto the spatula and place it on the sides of the cake. Smooth it out slightly and continue to do this all the way around the cake while turning the turntable with your left hand. As you cover each area, rotate the turntable. When all of the sides are iced, place your spatula on the side of the cake and spread and turn the cake until the icing is smooth all around.

Place coconut on a sheet of wax paper. Lift the cake in your left hand and stick coconut to the sides of the cake with your right hand, slowly. Be sure to cover all sides. Set the cake down and sprinkle coconut on the top. Serve cake at room temperature. It will keep for up to 5 days.

LEMON SQUARES

▪▪

I am particularly proud of the fact that my lemon squares are not only delicious but beautiful. It's hard to improve on these beautifully shiny yellow squares. The squares have one drawback; while they're baking a white foam floats to the top and must be removed. My employee Miguel is great at this painstaking job. His patience and doggedness have made my glossy lemon squares a consistent bestseller. Muchas gracias, Miguel!

MAKES 6 (3-INCH) SQUARES

Bottom crust:
1 cup unsalted butter at room temperature
½ cup confectioners' sugar
2 cups all-purpose flour

Filling:
9 extra-large eggs
3 cups granulated sugar
1½ cups pure lemon juice

Make crust:
Preheat oven to 350°F. Spray a 12 x 9 x 3-inch pan. To make the crust, place all ingredients in the bowl of an electric mixer and beat until a ball is formed. Remove dough from the bowl and press into the bottom of the baking pan to form one even layer. Place pan in the oven and bake for 10 to 15 minutes until the crust is very slightly brown. While crust is baking, prepare the filling.

Make filling:
Break eggs into a small bowl and add them to bowl of electric mixer. Add the sugar and beat until well combined. Add in the lemon juice and beat on a low speed. When bottom crust is done, place the pan on the counter and pour the lemon liquid through a fine strainer over the crust. Carefully place pan back in the oven. After about 4 to 5 minutes, carefully pull out the oven rack the lemon squares are on. With a flat plastic scraper carefully pull as much white foam as you can toward the edge of the pan and remove it. Then carefully push the oven rack back and allow the lemon square to continue to bake. Do this one or two more times. You must do it before the liquid has solidified. Once it is hard you cannot remove the foam. Bake until completely solidified with no jiggling in the middle. Baking should take approximately 15 to 20 minutes, but you must watch carefully. Allow to cool completely. Cut it into squares with a thin, long knife. Run a bench scraper around the edges to loosen them before taking out the first square with an offset spatula. The lemon squares will keep up to 5 days well wrapped in the refrigerator.

CHAPTER FIVE

OUR HOUSE

LINZER TARTS

In my dreams, I sit in a coffee shop in Vienna drinking coffee mitt schlag (with whipped cream) and eating a piece of linzer torte—ground almonds with cinnamon, cocoa, and raspberry jam in perfect harmony. We use this dough to make linzer cookies, a sandwich of two cookies with raspberry jam in the middle. We also make linzer squares by pressing the dough into a cookie sheet, spreading the top with raspberry jam, and piping a lattice on top. Almost Vienna!

MAKES ABOUT 24 (2½-INCH) TARTS

2 cups all-purpose flour

2 cups toasted almonds, finely ground

2 tbsp. cocoa powder

1 tbsp. cinnamon

1 cup unsalted butter at room temperature

1 cup granulated sugar

1 tbsp. pure vanilla extract

2 extra-large egg yolks

1½ cups raspberry jam with seeds

For linzer tarts, you must chill the dough before using. Measure flour, almonds, cocoa, and cinnamon in a bowl. In the bowl of an electric mixer, beat the butter and sugar until well combined. Add the vanilla and egg yolks and beat until thoroughly incorporated. Add the dry ingredients to the electric mixer and beat on low speed. When all the flour is incorporated, raise the speed and beat for 1 minute. Remove the dough from the bowl, wrap in plastic wrap, and chill for at least 2 hours or overnight.

Preheat oven to 350°F. Spray a 10 x 15-inch cookie sheet or line it with parchment. Remove dough from the refrigerator and cut in half. Return the other piece to the refrigerator. Cut the dough into several pieces with a bench scraper and then pull them together again, forming a smooth ball. Place dough on a floured surface and flour the top of the dough. With a traditional rolling pin, roll away from yourself, constantly turning the dough, until you have rolled it out to ¼-inch thick. Cut the dough into circles with a scalloped edge cutter. Fill the cookie sheet. The cookies should be close but not touching. Cut out a small circle in the middle of half of the cookies. Place in oven and bake for 12 to 15 minutes or until the cookies are firm to the touch. They will not brown. Allow to cool. Spread a thin layer of jam on the flat cookies. Place cutout cookies on wax paper and sprinkle them with confectioners' sugar. Now sandwich the two halves of the cookies. These cookies have a great shelf life, and are delicious for up to 10 days stored in an airtight container.

LINZER SQUARES

▄▃▂▃▄▃▂▃▄▃▂▃▄▃▂▃▄▃▂▃▄▃▂▃▄▃▂▃▄▃▂▃▄▃▂▃▄▃▂▃▄▃▂▃▄▃▂▃▄▃▂▃▄▃▂▃

I started to make the linzer squares when we had dough leftover from the linzer tarts. It would get very dry and hard to roll. I softened the dough with an extra egg, pressed it into a pan, spread the raspberry jam, piped out the lines, and I had a new product.

MAKES 12 (3-INCH) SQUARES

2 cups all-purpose flour

2 cups toasted almonds, finely ground

2 tbsp. cocoa powder

1 tbsp. cinnamon

1 cup unsalted butter at room temperature

1 cup granulated sugar

1 tbsp. pure vanilla extract

2 extra-large egg yolks

1 extra-large egg

½ tsp. baking powder

1½ cups raspberry jam with seeds

Preheat oven to 350°F. Spray a 12 x 9 x 3-inch pan. Measure flour, almonds, cocoa, and cinnamon in a bowl. In the bowl of an electric mixer, beat the butter and sugar until well combined. Add the vanilla and egg yolks and beat until thoroughly incorporated. Add the dry ingredients to the electric mixer and beat on low speed. When all the flour is incorporated, raise the speed and beat for 1 minute. Add in egg and baking powder to make the dough easier to press into the pan and pipe through the pastry bag. Remove half the dough from the mixer and press into prepared pan; it should be ½-inch thick and come halfway up the sides of the pan. Spread raspberry jam on the surface of the dough. Place some of the dough in a 12-inch pastry bag with coupler. Pipe lines on top of jam ½-inch apart. You can pipe on a diagonal or straight up and down. Make the same number of lines in both directions so the top has a lattice pattern. Place in the oven and bake for 20 to 25 minutes or until the top feels firm. Allow to cool. Linzer squares will keep up to 2 weeks in an airtight container.

PEANUT BUTTER COOKIES

This recipe was inspired by McCall's Magazine Cookbook, a fun, old-fashioned cookbook with very few pictures and recipes for dishes like creamed chicken on toast. I made some adjustments to turn this into a great peanut butter cookie. You can either make them jumbo-size like we do in the store or bite-size with fork marks, a traditional decoration.

MAKES 24–30 COOKIES

1¼ cups all-purpose flour
¾ tsp. baking soda
½ tsp. baking powder
¼ tsp. salt
½ cup unsalted butter at room temperature

½ cup peanut butter
½ cup granulated sugar
½ cup brown sugar
1 extra-large egg

Preheat oven to 350°F. Spray a 10 x 15-inch cookie sheet or line with parchment. Measure flour, baking soda, baking powder, and salt in a bowl. Beat butter and peanut butter in the bowl of an electric mixer until combined. Add sugars and beat well. Break egg into a cup and add to mixer. Slowly add dry ingredients to the electric mixer. When incorporated, raise the speed and beat for 30 seconds. Form dough into balls the size of ping pong balls. Eight should fit on the cookie sheet and give the cookies room to spread. Press tines of fork down on each cookie, first one direction then the other. Bake for 12 to 15 minutes or until lightly brown and cracked on top. Allow to cool. Bake all dough or store in a plastic container in the refrigerator for up to 2 weeks or freezer for up to 3 months.

CHOCOLATE CHOCOLATE-CHIP COOKIES

These cookies are a logical step after regular chocolate chip cookies. For people who can never get enough chocolate, this cookie is an intensely chocolate experience. Adding cream makes them taste even more chocolatey. They are a favorite of my daughter Katie—I always save one for her.

MAKES 24–30 COOKIES

1 cup unsalted butter at room temperature
½ cup brown sugar
1 cup granulated sugar
2 tbsp. heavy cream
½ tsp. pure vanilla extract

1¾ cup all-purpose flour
¼ tsp. baking soda
5 tbsp. cocoa powder
1 cup chopped walnuts
1 cup semisweet chocolate chips

Preheat oven to 350°F. Line a 10 x 15-inch cookie sheet with parchment or spray with pan release spray. In the bowl of an electric mixer beat the butter at medium speed until light and fluffy. Add both sugars and continue to beat until well combined. Add the cream and vanilla. In a separate bowl measure the flour, baking soda, and cocoa powder (if the cocoa powder is lumpy put it through a strainer before adding it to the flour). Add the flour mixture to the mixing bowl with mixer on low speed. Then add the walnuts and chocolate chips and beat until all ingredients are well combined. Form the dough into balls the size of a ping pong ball. If the dough is too soft, you can chill it for 30 minutes. Do not crowd the cookie sheet as the cookies will spread. You can fit about 8 to 12 cookies on a regular cookie sheet. Bake the cookies for 12 to 15 minutes. It is hard to tell when chocolate cookies are done. You will know when the top looks cracked and is somewhat firm to the touch. They taste better a little underbaked. Allow to cool and store cookies in an airtight container. Extra dough can be stored in a plastic container in the refrigerator for 2 weeks or frozen for up to 6 months.

GINGER COOKIES

▪▫

This ginger cookie recipe comes after much experimentation. My version creates a slightly sweet but chewy mouthful. I like rolling the uncooked dough in raw sugar—the result is a beautiful crunch plus a sparkle.

MAKES 24–30 COOKIES

1½ cups unsalted butter at room
    temperature
1 cup granulated sugar
1 cup brown sugar
1 extra-large egg
½ cup molasses

4 cups flour
1½ tsp. ginger
1½ tsp.cinnamon
1 tbsp. baking soda
½ tsp. salt
½ cup raw sugar

Preheat oven to 350°F. Line a 10 x 15-inch cookie sheet with parchment or spray. In the bowl of an electric mixer beat the butter and sugars until well combined. Break egg in a cup and add to mixer with the molasses and beat on slow speed. Measure flour, ginger, cinnamon, baking soda, and salt in a mixing bowl and add to mixer. Beat until flour is completely incorporated. Place the raw sugar in a shallow bowl. Form the dough into balls the size of ping pong balls and roll them in the raw sugar and place them on the cookie sheet. Eight should fit on the cookie sheet and give the cookies room to spread. Bake 12 to 15 minutes or until cookies are still slightly soft to the touch. Allow to cool. Repeat with remaining dough. Store in the refrigerator for up to 2 weeks or in the freezer for up to 3 months.

GRANOLA COOKIES

We started to make our own granola to use in this cookie. This is really a granola bar masquerading as a cookie. The ingredients are all healthy and very filling—perfect to pack for your hiking trip.

MAKES 18–24 COOKIES

1 cup unsalted butter at room temperature

¾ cup brown sugar

1 extra-large egg

3 cups granola (see homemade
   recipe on pg. 129)

1 cup all-purpose flour

½ tsp. salt

¾ cup raisins

½ cup sliced almonds

½ cup coconut

½ cup peanuts

Preheat oven to 350°F. Spray a 10 x 15-inch cookie sheet or line it with parchment. Place butter and brown sugar in the bowl of an electric mixer and beat until combined. Break egg into a cup, add it to the mixer, and beat. Measure granola, flour, salt, raisins, almonds, coconut, and peanuts in a bowl and add it to the mixer. Beat on low speed only until all ingredients are combined. Form the dough into ping pong size balls and place on cookie sheet. Up to 12 cookies will fit on the cookie sheet. These cookies do not spread. Bake for 12 to 15 minutes or until cookies are firm and lightly brown. Allow to cool. Bake all the dough or place in a plastic container and refrigerate for up to 2 weeks or freeze for up to 3 months.

ALMOND BISCOTTI

I started making biscotti because a customer asked for them. First, I made almond biscotti, then somebody wanted chocolate, until pretty soon I was making four kinds of biscotti. Fortunately, my father (always on a low cholesterol diet) could eat biscotti. He was a helpful consumer of leftover biscotti. My uncle Tony was also helpful—he liked to dunk anything—no matter how stale the biscotti got! Neither my father nor Tony are around anymore, but I've fortunately got other loyal biscotti customers.

MAKES 12–14 BISCOTTI

2 cups all-purpose flour
¾ cup granulated sugar
1½ cups sliced almonds
½ tsp. baking soda

½ tsp. baking powder
¼ tsp. salt
3 extra-large eggs
1 tsp. pure vanilla extract

Preheat oven to 350°F. Line a 10 x 15-inch cookie sheet with parchment paper or spray. Combine flour, sugar, almonds, baking soda, baking powder, and salt in the bowl of an electric mixer. Mix on slow speed to combine. Break eggs in a small bowl, add vanilla, pour into mixer bowl, and beat until the mixture comes together in a ball. Turn the ball out on a lightly floured surface. Form the dough into a log by rolling and stretching it on a floured work surface. The log should be a little shorter than the length of your cookie sheet. Lift the log onto the cookie sheet and flatten it into a 9 x 6-inch rectangle. Bake for 15 to 20 minutes or until it is firm and lightly brown. Remove from oven and allow to cool. When cool, carefully lift the rectangle onto a cutting board and with a long serrated knife, slice the rectangle on a diagonal in ¼-inch slices. The first slices on either end of the log will be shorter than the slices in the middle, which should be uniform in length. Put the slices on the parchment–lined cookie sheet and return to oven for 10 to 12 minutes to brown lightly. Allow to cool. Store in an airtight container for up to 1 month.

CHOCOLATE BISCOTTI

Biscotti are one of my weaknesses. I love this recipe as well as the chocolate chip pistachio recipe. When we attend a food show I only find biscotti samples in my bag when we get home. A tin of biscotti guarantees you will always have something to serve if someone drops in for coffee. They have a great shelf life.

MAKES 24 BISCOTTI

2 cups all-purpose flour

2 cups sliced almonds

⅓ cup cocoa powder

½ cup granulated sugar

½ cup brown sugar

⅓ cup semi-sweet chocolate chips

½ tsp. baking soda

½ tsp. baking powder

¼ tsp. salt

3 extra-large eggs

1 tsp. pure vanilla extract

Preheat oven to 350 °F. Line two 10 x 15-inch cookie sheets with parchment. Place flour, almonds, cocoa, sugars, chocolate chips, baking soda, baking powder, and salt in the bowl of an electric mixer. Beat on low speed until combined. Break eggs into a small bowl and add vanilla. Pour into bowl of electric mixer and beat until it just forms a ball. Turn out onto lightly floured surface and divide into two pieces. Roll each piece into a fat log about 7 inches long and place on the cookie sheet. Flatten the log into an 8 x 6-inch rectangle (flour your hands if the dough feels sticky). Do the same with the other piece. Place in oven and bake for 15 to 17 minutes until it is firm to the touch. Remove from oven and allow to cool. Carefully transfer the rectangle to a cutting board and slice it on a diagonal in ¼-inch slices. The first slices on either end of the log will be shorter than the slices in the middle, which should be uniform in length. Place the slices on the parchment-lined cookie sheet, do the same thing to the other rectangle of dough, and return both to the oven for 10 to 12 minutes. They should be slightly browned, although it can hard to tell with chocolate cookies. Allow to cool. Store in an airtight container for up to 1 month.

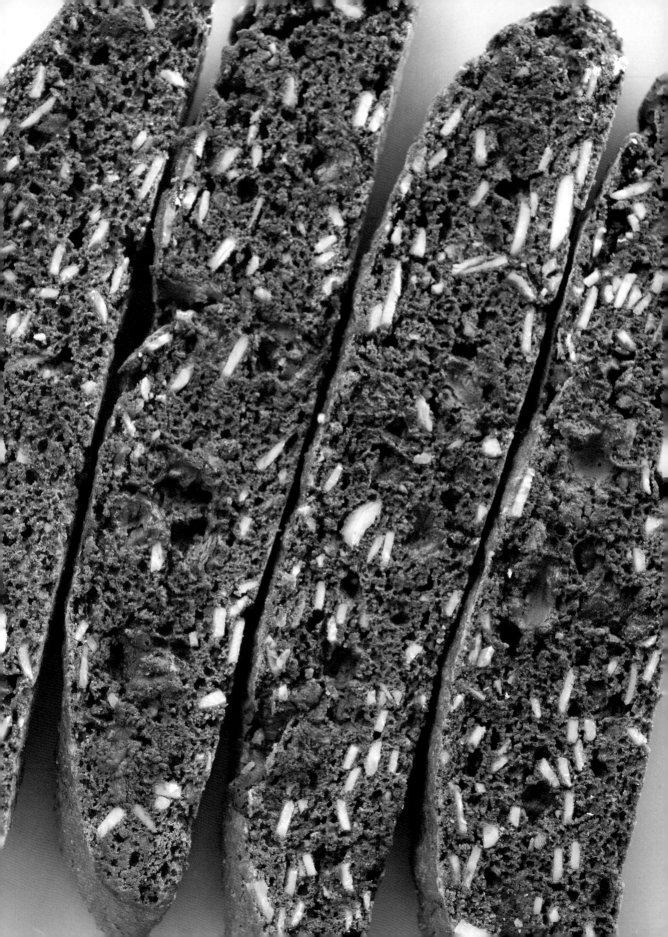

CRANBERRY CHIP PISTACHIO BISCOTTI

These are slightly richer than the other biscotti, not only because the ingredients are costlier, but because they have butter in them. This makes a softer biscotti—a lot easier on the teeth.

MAKES 16–24 BISCOTTI

2 cups all-purpose flour

1½ cups granulated sugar

½ tsp. baking soda

½ tsp. baking powder

¼ tsp. salt

½ cup unsalted butter, chilled

½ cup dried cranberries or dried cherries

½ cup semi-sweet chocolate chips

½ cup pistachios

3 extra-large eggs

1 tsp. pure vanilla extract

Preheat oven to 350°F. Line two 10 x 15-inch cookie sheets with parchment or spray. In the bowl of an electric mixer combine flour, sugar, baking soda, baking powder, and salt. Beat on low speed, cut butter into small pieces and add to mixer and beat until the butter is incorporated with the flour (until no big pieces are visible). Add the cherries or cranberries, chocolate chips, and pistachios and mix to combine. Break the eggs into a small bowl, add the vanilla, add into mixer bowl, and beat until a ball forms. Turn dough out onto lightly floured surface. Divide into two pieces. Form each piece into an 8-inch long log and place on the prepared cookie sheets. Press logs down to form a 6 x 8-inch rectangle (wet your hands if the dough feels sticky). Place both cookie sheets in the oven and bake for 15 to 18 minutes or until lightly brown and firm to the touch. Allow to cool. Carefully place rectangle onto a cutting board and slice it on a diagonal. The first slices on either end of the log will be shorter than the slices in the middle, which should be uniform in length. Place biscotti slices back on parchment–lined cookie sheets and bake again for 10 to 12 minutes until the slices are dry and lightly brown. Allow to cool. Store in an airtight container for 1 week.

APPLE CRUMB SQUARES

If you don't want to make squares, you can also put this recipe in a pie shell; both are delicious served warm with vanilla ice cream. I make large batches of these apple squares. Though I prefer working on a smaller scale, a large sheet pan lined with pie dough and mounded up with apples and covered with crumbs is very exhilarating. I picture one of my oldest employees, Sarah Solis, with a giant pile of apples in front of her. She is creating a work of art! She's peeled, cored, and cubed the apples, is placing them in the pan, neatly sprinkling on the crumbs. Thumbs up, Sarah!

MAKES 12 (3-INCH) SQUARES OR 8 (10-INCH) PIE SLICES

Pâte brisée (pie dough):
3 cups all-purpose flour
2 tbsp. granulated sugar
¼ tsp. salt
½ cup unsalted butter,
     well chilled
½ cup vegetable
     shortening, well chilled
½ cup ice water

Filling:
6–7 Granny Smith apples
½ cup brown sugar
1 tbsp. all-purpose flour
¼ tsp. salt
1 tsp. cinnamon
1 tsp. lemon juice
½ cup sour cream

Crumb topping:
2 cups walnuts
2⅓ cups all-purpose flour
6 tbsp. granulated sugar
6 tbsp. brown sugar
1 tsp. cinnamon
½ cup unsalted butter,
     chilled

Make pâte brisée (pie dough):
Put the flour, sugar, and salt in bowl of a food processor with metal blade. Cut butter and shortening into small pieces and add it to bowl. Pulse mixture until the butter is completely combined with flour. With food processor running, slowly pour in ice water. The mixture should just come together—you don't want it to be sticky. Crumbly is fine. Turn dough out on floured surface and pull dough together with your hands to form ball. If it seems dry, sprinkle a few drops of water directly on dough. Wrap dough in plastic wrap and refrigerate for at least 2 hours. Remove dough from the refrigerator and place ball of dough on floured work surface and press it down. Lightly flour top of the dough. Use a traditional rolling pin. Put rolling pin in the middle of dough and start rolling away from you. Turn dough a little at a time in a clockwise direction and roll again until you have a circle about 10 inches in diameter. Place dough in 9-inch pie plate and make a decorative edge. If you are making squares, roll the dough into a 10 x 13-inch rectangle and place in a 12 x 9 x 3-inch pan. Place pan or pie plate in the refrigerator while you prepare the apples and the crumbs.

Continued on next page

Make filling:

Peel, core, and cut apples into big chunks; you should have about 4 cups of apples. Put the apples into a large mixing bowl, add all the rest of the filling ingredients, and toss to combine.

Make crumb topping:

In the bowl of a food processor put the nuts, flour, sugars, cinnamon, and butter cut into small pieces. Pulse the mixture until all the butter is mixed in and mixture is crumbly.

Make squares:

Preheat oven to 350°F. Take pie plate or baking pan out of the refrigerator and pile the apples into it. Cover the apples with the crumbs, place in the oven, and bake for 55 to 60 minutes. The crumbs should be well browned and the apples should be very juicy. You may need to put a larger pan underneath the pie or sheet pan to catch the liquid so it won't drip into the oven. Allow to cool completely. This will keep in the refrigerator for 4 days.

CREAM CHEESE BROWNIES

▪▪

These brownies have been in my life for a very long time. I love to make them and I never get tired of swirling the chocolate into the cream cheese. My aunt in California used to ask me to send her two. She would cut them into quarters so she could enjoy small bites every night as a treat. They are a decadent, gratifying indulgence.

MAKES 18 BROWNIES

Brownie batter:

5 oz. semi-sweet chocolate

5 oz. unsweetened chocolate

1 cup unsalted butter

4 extra-large eggs

1 cup brown sugar

1 cup granulated sugar

¾ tsp. pure vanilla extract

1¼ cups all-purpose flour

¾ tsp. baking powder

¼ tsp. salt

¼ cup chopped walnuts

Cream cheese filling:

6 tbsp. unsalted butter at room temperature

12 oz. cream cheese at room temperature

1 cup granulated sugar

½ tsp. pure vanilla extract

3 extra-large eggs

Make batter:

Preheat oven to 350°F. Spray a 12 x 9 x 3-inch baking pan. Place chocolates and butter in a metal bowl and place in the oven to melt. Check the chocolate frequently, carefully removing the bowl from the oven and stirring until the chocolate is completely melted. In the bowl of an electric mixer beat the eggs, sugars, and vanilla until combined. Add the melted chocolate and butter to the ingredients in the mixer and beat until combined. Measure the flour, baking powder, and salt, slowly add it to the rest of the ingredients, and beat until everything is well combined. Scoop out about 2 cups of the batter, place in a bowl, and set aside. (Place bowl on a warm spot on your stove, if you have one, to keep the chocolate soft). Add the nuts to the mixer and beat to combine. Pour batter into prepared pan and with an offset spatula smooth the batter to make one even layer.

Continued on next page

Make filling:

Beat butter and cream cheese in the bowl of an electric mixer. Add sugar and vanilla and beat until smooth. Break eggs in a cup and add them to the mixer beating on medium speed for about 5 minutes. Scrape the bowl with a rubber scraper. Pour the cream cheese mixture on top of the brownie layer and even it with a spatula. Take the chocolate you have set aside and drop large spoonfuls randomly on top of the cream cheese. Swirl the chocolate around with a knife. Place in the oven and bake 45 to 50 minutes or until the top of the cream cheese is lightly brown and firm to the touch. Allow to cool completely. Brownies will keep up to 10 days stored in an airtight container.

DATE NUT BARS

I have been making these bars for years—they are like old friends. Beautiful Medjool dates are always in our Christmas gift baskets. One year we overordered and this date nut bar came to the rescue. Cooking apples with the dates makes the filling less dense. The smell in the kitchen when you are making these bars is wonderful.

MAKES 9 BARS

5 cups pitted dates, coarsely chopped

4 apples peeled, cored, chopped in food processor

3 tbsp. water

3 tbsp. granulated sugar

1½ cups + 6 tbsp. unsalted butter

1½ cups + 6 tbsp. brown sugar

4½ cups all-purpose flour

1½ tsp. cinnamon

1½ tsp. salt

2 cups walnuts, finely chopped

Put the dates, apples, water, and sugar in a saucepan, place over medium heat, and cover the pot. Cook for 35 to 40 minutes, stirring often until the mixture is soft and the consistency of thick applesauce. Set aside. Preheat oven to 350°F. Spray a 12 x 9 x 3-inch pan. In the bowl of an electric mixer beat the butter and brown sugar until well combined. Measure the flour, cinnamon, salt, and walnuts in a bowl. On low speed add the dry ingredients and beat until the flour is incorporated but the mixture is still crumbly. Do not overbeat or you will not have the crumbs needed for the topping. Press half the crumb mixture in the prepared pan, forming one even layer. Top with the date and apple mixture and spread evenly. Place remaining crumb mixture on top of the date and apple layer. Place in oven and bake for 40 to 45 minutes. Top will be brown and firm to the touch. Allow to cool completely. Bars keep for up to 1 week in an airtight container.

COCONUT CHOCOLATE CHIP BARS

∎∎

These are a favorite of mine. I hunt for crumbs in the pan after the bars have been packed for customers. They are most delicious when they are slightly warm—I recommend microwaving one for a couple of seconds before you eat it.

MAKES 9 BARS

Crust:
1 cup unsalted butter at room temperature
½ cup confectioners' sugar
2 cups all-purpose flour

Filling:
1½ cups unsalted butter at room temperature
1½ cups brown sugar
3 extra-large eggs
1 tsp. pure vanilla extract
½ cup all-purpose flour
1½ cups chopped walnuts
2 cups sweetened coconut flakes
3 cups semi-sweet chocolate chips

Make crust:

Preheat oven to 350°F. Spray a 9 x 6 x 3-inch pan. Place butter, sugar, and flour in the bowl of an electric mixer and beat until the ingredients are well combined and form a ball. Press dough in the prepared pan and place in oven for 12 to 15 minutes or until just beginning to brown.

Make filling:

While crust is baking, place butter and brown sugar in bowl of electric mixer and beat until smooth. Break eggs into a cup and add them to the mixer with the vanilla and beat until all ingredients are incorporated. In a separate bowl combine flour, walnuts, coconut flakes, and chocolate chips and add them to the mixer, beating on low speed until mixture is well combined. Spread mixture on prepared crust. Bake for 55 to 60 minutes until top is brown. Allow to cool completely. Bars can be stored in an airtight container for up to 1 week.

CHOCOLATE CHIP BROWNIES

Everybody thinks their brownie recipe makes the "best brownie in the world." I bake several kinds of brownies, hoping to please as many customers as possible. But this recipe with no nuts became my basic brownie a long time ago. No recipe can have too many chocolate chips so I put them in the batter, giving the brownies a crunchy texture and more intense chocolate flavor. I guess I'm doing something right because the Walt Disney Publishing Co. named it Best Brownie on the Planet 2004! I have a certificate to prove it. I hope this will become your new favorite brownie.

MAKES 12 (3-INCH) BROWNIES

4 ounces unsweetened chocolate

10 ounces semi-sweet chocolate

1 cup + 4 tbsp. unsalted butter

2 cups granulated sugar

7 extra-large eggs

1 tsp. pure vanilla extract

2 cups all-purpose flour

½ tsp. salt

2 cups semi-sweet chocolate chips

Preheat oven to 350°F. Spray a 9 x 12 x 3-inch pan. Place chocolates and butter in a metal bowl and place in the oven to melt. Stir every 4 to 5 minutes until completely melted. In the bowl of an electric mixer place sugar, eggs, and vanilla and beat until well combined. Add melted chocolate mixture and mix well. Add the flour, salt, and chocolate chips and beat on low speed until just combined. Pour batter in prepared pan. Bake for 45 to 50 minutes or until the center of the brownies are firm to the touch. If the brownies are beginning to rise they will be overbaked. Allow to cool. Store brownies in an airtight container up to 1 week.

RASPBERRY BROWNIES

Raspberries and chocolate go well together, which makes these raspberry brownies so great. If you have a brownie recipe you love, you can improvise. This is a brownie with a similar beginning but an unexpected ending.

MAKES 18 BROWNIES

5 oz. semi-sweet chocolate

5 oz. unsweetened chocolate

1 cup unsalted butter

4 extra-large eggs

1 cup granulated sugar

1 cup brown sugar

¾ tsp. pure vanilla extract

1¼ cups all-purpose flour

¾ tsp. baking powder

¼ tsp. salt

¼ cup chopped walnuts

1½ cups seeded raspberry preserves

Preheat oven 350°F. Spray a 9 x 12 x 3-inch baking pan. Place semi-sweet chocolate, unsweetened chocolate, and butter in a metal bowl in the oven to melt. Check every 5 minutes, stirring until completely melted. Place eggs, sugars, and vanilla in bowl of electric mixer and beat until well combined. Add melted chocolate to egg mixture and stir on low speed to combine. Measure flour, baking powder, and salt in a bowl and add to mixer bowl. Beat until all ingredients are incorporated. Scoop out 2 cups of batter and place in bowl you used to melt the chocolate. Add walnuts to remaining batter and stir. Pour rest of batter into prepared pan and spread in one even layer. Put raspberry jam in separate bowl and stir with spoon to soften, then spread jam on top of brownie batter with offset spatula. Pour the 2 cups of reserved batter on top of jam and spread carefully to completely cover jam. Place in oven and bake 45 to 55 minutes or until center is firm to the touch. Allow to cool. Brownies be stored in an airtight container for up to 1 week.

CHOCOLATE CAKE

■▪■

Every baker has a chocolate cake recipe. I have changed my chocolate cake recipe several times since I started baking professionally, but have realized that you can't please everyone, so here's the cake I love. I have made many birthday cakes with this recipe and it also makes a delicious loaf cake and cupcakes.

MAKES 1 (10-INCH) CAKE, SERVES 25 PEOPLE, 2 (9-INCH) LOAF CAKES, SERVES 16–18 SLICES, OR 24 CUPCAKES

Cake:

6 oz. semi-sweet chocolate

¼ cup cocoa powder

1 cup water

1½ cups unsalted butter at room temperature

2 cups granulated sugar

1 tsp. pure vanilla extract

6 extra-large eggs

3½ cups all-purpose flour

1½ tsp. baking soda

½ tsp. salt

1½ cups sour cream

Chocolate buttercream:

1 cup unsalted butter at room temperature

½ tsp. pure vanilla extract

2 tbsp. heavy cream

3 cups confectioners' sugar

6 tbsp. cocoa powder

Make cake:

Preheat oven to 350°F. Spray 2 (10-inch) layer pans and line them with parchment paper or 2 (9-inch) loaf pans or 24 (½-cup) cupcake cups. Put semi-sweet chocolate, cocoa powder, and water in a small metal bowl and place in oven to melt chocolate. It takes about 10 minutes for the chocolate mixture to melt in the oven, but check after 2 to 3 minutes and stir. (This can also be done in a microwave oven in a plastic bowl for 30 seconds.) When chocolate is completely melted, whisk the mixture to eliminate any cocoa lumps and set aside. Cream butter in the bowl of an electric mixer, add granulated sugar and vanilla, and beat until well combined. Break eggs in a cup and add them to the mixer. Beat until incorporated, scraping the bowl down with a rubber spatula. Measure flour, baking soda, and salt in a bowl, add to mixer beating on low speed, then add sour cream and beat until smooth. Add in melted chocolate mixture and mix until completely incorporated. Pour into prepared pans and bake for 45 to 50 minutes or until cake is firm to the touch

Continued on next page

and a thin knife comes out clean. Allow to cool completely. (If you are decorating a birthday cake or occasion cake follow directions on pg. 69.)

Make buttercream:

In the bowl of the electric mixer beat butter until light and fluffy, add vanilla and heavy cream, and beat until combined. Slowly add confectioners' sugar to the bowl. When sugar is incorporated, add cocoa powder. If cocoa is lumpy, sift it before adding to the buttercream. Beat until mixture is a smooth, spreadable consistency.

BLACKOUT CHOCOLATE CAKE

▪▪▪

When I first moved to Brooklyn people talked about a well-known and beloved bakery called Ebingers. It had closed by the time I got there. Ebingers was famous for blackout chocolate cake. With my own version of this classic and unforgettable blackout chocolate cake, here's to Ebingers.

MAKES 1 (10-INCH) ROUND CAKE, SERVES 25 PEOPLE

Cake:

6 oz. semi-sweet chocolate

¼ cup cocoa powder

1 cup water

1½ cups unsalted butter at
   room temperature

2 cups granulated sugar

1 tsp. pure vanilla extract

6 extra-large eggs

3½ cups all-purpose flour

1½ tsp. baking soda

½ tsp. salt

1½ cups sour cream

Glaze:

1 pound semi-sweet
   chocolate

¾ cups dark corn syrup

½ cup water

8 tbsp. butter

Make cake:

Preheat oven to 350°F. Spray 2 (10-inch) layer pans and line with parchment paper. Put semi-sweet chocolate, cocoa powder, and water in small metal bowl and place in oven to melt chocolate. It takes about 10 minutes for chocolate mixture to melt in oven, but check after 2 to 3 minutes and stir. (This can be done in a microwave oven in a plastic bowl for with 30 seconds.) When chocolate is completely melted, whisk mixture to eliminate any cocoa lumps and set aside. Cream butter in bowl of an electric mixer, add granulated sugar and vanilla, and beat until well combined. Break eggs in cup and add to mixer. Beat until incorporated, scraping bowl down with a rubber spatula. Measure flour, baking soda, and salt in a bowl and add to mixer beating on low speed, then add sour cream and beat until smooth. Add melted chocolate mixture and mix until completely incorporated. Pour into prepared pans and bake for 45 to 50 minutes or until cake is firm to the touch and a thin knife comes out clean. Allow to cool completely.

Make glaze:

Put all ingredients in large metal bowl and place in oven until melted. Stir every 5 minutes for 15 to 20 minutes until completely melted. When melted, stir mixture until smooth and shiny. Pour half of mixture into bowl and put in freezer for 10 to 15 minutes. Stir occasionally until a spreadable consistency is reached. Keep other half of mixture in warm spot on the oven.

Continued on next page

Assemble cake:

Cut out a cardboard circle the same size as cake. Remove one layer from pan, peel off parchment paper, and place on cardboard circle. Take a long serrated knife and level the top of the cake by placing the knife horizontally against the side of the cake and turning the cake as you cut. Split cake layer using the same technique. Do not remove parchment from second layer but level top and split layer in half. Put cake trimmings in food processor with metal blade. Separate all four layers. With an offset spatula spread ½-inch chilled glaze on bottom layer and top with next layer. Repeat with next two layers. Peel parchment paper off top layer. Place cake in freezer for 30 minutes. Put cake on a wire rack over a sheet pan and pour warm glaze over the entire cake. Tilt rack to make sure glaze is covering sides of cake completely. Let cake set for about 5 minutes. Chop cake trimmings in food processor and turn out on sheet of wax paper. With cake in your left hand (if you are right handed) grab a handful of crumbs. Press crumbs into side of cake with your right hand, turning cake after each crumb application. When you have covered the cake with crumbs, place on serving plate. Leftover glaze can be reused for your next blackout cake. Store in plastic container in refrigerator for up to 1 month.

GERMAN CHOCOLATE CAKE

This cake is super gooey delicious. It's hard to resist tasting the filling—you will have to exercise restraint to be sure it makes it into the cake! Use the filling as soon as it's made; it will drip down the sides of the chilled cake like lava.

MAKES 2 (10-INCH) CHOCOLATE CAKE LAYERS, SERVES 25 PEOPLE

Pecan coconut filling:

1 cup heavy cream

1 cup granulated sugar

½ cup unsalted butter

3 extra-large egg yolks

1 tsp. pure vanilla extract

1 cup chopped pecans

1⅓ cups sweetened coconut flakes

Chocolate buttercream:

1 cup unsalted butter at room temperature

½ tsp. pure vanilla extract

2 tbsp. heavy cream

3 cups confectioners' sugar

6 tbsp. cocoa powder

Make filling:

Put heavy cream, sugar, and butter in a small saucepan over medium heat. Cook over medium heat until sugar has dissolved and butter is melted. In a small bowl, whisk egg yolks, adding the cream mixture a little at a time, whisking constantly. Return yolk mixture to saucepan and cook until it has thickened. Remove from heat and add vanilla, pecans, and coconut. Allow to cool.

Make buttercream:

In the bowl of an electric mixer beat butter until light and fluffy, add vanilla and heavy cream, and beat until combined. Slowly add confectioners' sugar to the bowl. When sugar is incorporated, add cocoa powder. If cocoa is lumpy, sift it before adding to the buttercream. Beat until mixture is a smooth spreading consistency.

Assemble cake:

Place one layer on a flat serving plate and level the top of the cake with a long serrated knife by cutting the top of the layer, turning the cake slightly as you cut to make the top an even layer. Then cut this layer in half using the same method, but starting in the middle of the layer. Repeat with the other layer. Separate the layers—you should have one layer on a serving plate and three on the work surface. Spread a thin layer of pecan coconut filling on the serving plate layer and top with another layer. Repeat with another layer. Place final layer on top and freeze the cake for

Continued on next page

45 minutes to 1 hour. Now, place the cake on a turntable. Place mixer bowl with buttercream on the left side of the turntable and remove paddle. With an offset spatula in your right hand, scoop icing onto the spatula and place it on the sides of the cake. Smooth it out all the way around the cake by turning the turntable with your left hand. Rotate the turntable as you cover each area. When sides are iced, place your spatula on the side of the cake and turn the cake until the icing is smoothed all around. Scoop some icing on top of the cake and smooth it neatly to the edges.

Chill the cake in the refrigerator for 30 minutes or 15 minutes in the freezer to harden icing. Remove cake and pour the rest of the pecan coconut filling over top of the cake. Push filling over the edges so it drips down the sides in a random fashion. If you are going to write on the cake you will need to chill it again. You can keep the cake for 1 day in the refrigerator but it tastes best at room temperature.

APPLE TARTS

These tarts do not have frangipane filling on the bottom. They have an apple filling and an apple topping. I used to slice the apples for the top of the tarts by hand, but now we have a slicing machine. You can slice the apples by hand but a mandolin will make the slices more uniform. With even slices placed decoratively on top, the tart will look beautiful, especially when it is glazed.

MAKES 6–8 SLICES

Pâte brisée (tart dough):
3 cups all-purpose flour
2 tbsp. granulated sugar
¼ tsp. salt
1 cup unsalted butter, well
    chilled
½ cup ice water

Filling:
4 large Granny Smith
    apples, peeled
⅓ cup granulated sugar
¼ tsp. cinnamon

Glaze:
1 cup apricot jam
1 tbsp. currants

Make pâte brisée (tart dough):
Put the flour, sugar, and salt in the bowl of a food processor with metal blade. Cut butter into small pieces and add it to the bowl. Pulse the mixture until the butter is completely combined with the flour. With the food processor running slowly, pour in the ice water. The mixture should just come together—you don't want it to be sticky. Crumbly is fine. Turn dough out on a floured surface and pull the dough together with your hands to form a ball. If it seems too dry, sprinkle a few drops of water directly on the dough. Wrap the dough in plastic wrap and refrigerate for at least 2 hours. Take the dough out of the refrigerator and divide it into 4 pieces. Each piece will fill an 8-inch tart shell. (Freeze or refrigerate other pieces of dough for another time.) Flour your work surface. Form the dough into a ball with your hands and place the ball of dough on the floured work surface and press it down. Lightly flour the top of the dough. Use a long, thin, tapered rolling pin. Put your rolling pin down in the middle of the dough and start rolling away from you. Turn the dough slightly in a clockwise direction and roll again. Keep doing this until you have a circle about 10 inches in diameter. Place the dough on top of the tart shell. With the heel of your hand remove the excess dough. It is now ready to fill.

Continued on next page

Make filling:

Preheat oven to 350°F. Cut 2 of the apples in half and core them. Cut the apples into small pieces and place in bowl of food processor and chop. Place chopped apples in a bowl and add sugar and cinnamon and mix well. Allow the apples to sit in the sugar until the liquid is released. Pick up the apples with your hands and squeeze out as much apple juice as you can. (You can also put the apples in a strainer and squeeze the juice out with the back of a large spoon). Put apple mixture into prepared tart shell. Press the apples down to cover the tart shell in an even layer. Cut the remaining 2 apples into quarters and remove the cores carefully. Slice the apples with the mandolin or by hand. Place the apple slices on top of the filling in a decorative manner to cover the entire top of tart. Lightly sprinkle top of tart with granulated sugar, as if you were using salt. Place in oven and bake for 45 to 50 minutes or until apple slices are brown. Allow to cool completely.

Make glaze:

Put apricot jam in a small saucepan. Place over medium heat and stir until jam becomes liquified. You want to use the liquid, not the fruit, for the glaze. Remove tart from outer ring of tart shell. Place tart on serving plate with its metal bottom (a way to prevent disasters). Before glazing the tart place currants in the center of the tart. With a pastry brush, carefully but generously apply the apricot jam to the apple slices. Spoon some glaze over the currants. Let cool.

BUCHE DE NOEL (YULE LOG)

My grandma and cousin Elly used to make a chocolate roll with whipped cream inside. My daughter Julie unfortunately never got to taste grandma's chocolate roll, but she loved Elly's. The chocolate roll for this recipe almost meets Julie's approval. My mother and I decorate the buche every year, adding something new as an amusement. Chocolate holly leaves are essential, as are Red Hots and any brand of sour power green apple candy straws—not to mention meringue mushrooms! Before you serve the buche, sprinkle the top with confectioners' sugar. An early snowfall.

MAKES 10–12 SERVINGS

Meringue mushrooms:
½ cup (4 eggs) egg whites
    at room temperature
½ tsp. cream of tartar
1½ cups granulated sugar
3 oz. semi-sweet chocolate
2 tbsp. cocoa powder

Chocolate roll:
6 extra-large eggs
    separated
¾ cup granulated sugar
1 tsp. pure vanilla extract
¼ cup all-purpose flour
⅓ cup cocoa powder
¼ tsp. salt

Whipped cream filling:
¾ cup heavy cream
2 tbsp. confectioners'
    sugar
¼ tsp. pure vanilla extract

Ganache for frosting:
1 cup heavy cream
8 oz. semi-sweet chocolate

Chocolate leaves:
½ cup white chocolate
    chips
Fresh holly leaves or rose
    leaves (they must be
    fresh or they will not
    work properly)

Decorations:
Sour power green apple
    candy straws
Spearmint Leaves sugar-
    coated jelly candies
Red Hots or other red
    candies
M&M's
Confectioners' sugar

Make meringue mushrooms:
Preheat oven to 200°F. Line a 10 x 15-inch cookie sheet with parchment. Fit a 12-inch pastry bag with coupler. In the bowl of an electric mixer place egg whites and cream of tartar and beat on high speed until beginning to foam and expand. Slowly add the sugar 1 to 2 tablespoons at a time,

Continued on next page

beating well after each addition. When all the sugar is added, beat until you have a shiny, stiff meringue. Fill the pastry bag ¾ full of meringue. Make the caps of the mushrooms first by holding the pastry bag at a 45-degree angle with the tip very close to the pan and squeezing out a round disc about 1 inch in diameter. Gently pull the pastry bag away from the disc in an upward direction to avoid making a point. Repeat this process 12 to 15 times. The caps can be placed close together—they will not spread. To make the stems, fill the pastry bag about three quarters full and hold the pastry bag directly over the cookie sheet vertically and squeeze meringue out of the bag to create what looks like a tall white Hershey kiss. Make 12 to 15 of this shape and place them next to the caps on your cookie sheet. Place meringue in oven and bake for 2 hours. They will not brown but should be firm to the touch. Allow to cool. You can store the mushroom parts for up to three months in airtight container. To decorate the mushrooms, melt chocolate in the microwave. Pick up each mushroom cap and with a thin, sharp knife carefully make a small round hole in the bottom center of each. Then pick up each stem piece, dip it into the melted chocolate, and stick it into the hole in the cap. Repeat with all the stems and place the finished mushrooms stem-side down on the cookie sheet. Sprinkle cocoa powder through a fine sieve over the tops of the mushroom caps. Set aside your mushrooms. Do not discard the remaining melted chocolate— you will use it to make chocolate leaves.

Make chocolate roll:
Preheat oven to 350°F. Spray a 10 x 15-inch cookie sheet and line with parchment. Place egg yolks in the bowl of an electric mixer and add the granulated sugar and vanilla. Beat on medium speed until the mixture is light and fluffy. In a separate bowl, measure the flour, cocoa, and salt through a sieve and slowly add to the egg yolk mixture in the mixer bowl. Put batter into a large bowl and set aside. Clean the bowl of the electric mixer and attach the whisk. Now beat egg whites until soft peaks are formed. Add 1 cup of egg whites to the yolk and flour mixture to thin it. Gently fold the rest of the whites into the yolk and flour mixture. You want to incorporate the whites completely but keep them airy. Spread the mixture into the prepared pan—this will be a thin layer of batter. Place in oven and bake for 5 to 7 minutes until it is just set and slightly pulling away from the sides. Allow to cool completely. You will need a platter long enough to accommodate the roll and you will also need adequate space in the refrigerator or freezer for it.

Make filling:
Place all whipped cream filling ingredients in a small bowl. With a hand mixer (you can use an electric mixer with whisk), beat cream until light peaks form; do not overbeat. Remove chocolate roll from pan and place it horizontally in front of you. Spread the whipped cream on top with an offset spatula spreading to within ½ inch of the edges. With both hands, carefully pull away some of the parchment paper and begin to roll the cake into a log. Go very slowly, gently pulling away the paper as you roll. When it is completely rolled up, place it on a platter seam-side down and refrigerate for 2 hours or freeze for 1 hour.

Make ganache:
Heat heavy cream in a small saucepan over medium heat. Place chocolate in the bowl of a food processor and chop it into small pieces. When the heavy cream is barely simmering, slowly pour it into the food processor with the motor running. Beat the mixture until all the chocolate is melted. Pour into a bowl and refrigerate, stirring often. It needs to be chilled approximately 1 to 1½ hours) until it reaches spreading consistency. When the ganache can be spread, remove the roll from the refrigerator or freezer and spread the ganache all over the surface of the roll. Remember, this chocolate roll or yule log is a branch of a tree, so the surface need not be smooth. Turn the log to make sure you have covered both sides and ends. Place log in the refrigerator while you prepare the decorations.

Make chocolate leaves:
You will need two small, soft paint brushes and a parchment–lined cookie sheet. Melt the white chocolate chips in the microwave. Remove holly leaves and rose leaves from their stems and place them on the cookie sheet. You will need about 12 leaves in all and they can be various sizes. Hold a leaf in your left hand between your index finger and thumb to get as little chocolate on your hand as possible. Dip the brush into the melted chocolate (use what is left from making the meringue mushrooms) and spread it thickly on the underside of each leaf. When completely covered, replace on cookie sheet and repeat with all the leaves, making half with white chocolate and half with dark chocolate. Place the cookie sheet in the refrigerator until the chocolate has hardened. This will take 10 to 15 minutes.

Decorate the buche:
With clean scissors cut the sour power green apple candy straws in half and then in a few smaller lengths. Cut the spearmint leaves in half. Take the chocolate leaves out of the refrigerator and carefully remove the real leaves from the chocolate. Now decorate the buche in any way you like. You can refer to my photo for guidance in placing the Spearmint Leaves, Red Hots, and M&M's, but feel free to create your own version of the buche. Sprinkle confectioners' sugar on top when everything is in place. The buche will taste delicious for several days (if there is any left). Happy Holidays!

APPLE CRANBERRY TARTS

I keep frozen cranberries in our freezer all year round and don't consider them a seasonal ingredient. However, it may not be easy to find cranberries except around Thanksgiving time. Remember this recipe in the fall when cranberries are abundant everywhere. I first made these tarts for a lighter Thanksgiving dessert, but they were so popular I decided to make them available all the time.

MAKES 6–8 SERVINGS

Pâte brisée (tart dough):
3 cups all-purpose flour
2 tbsp. granulated sugar
¼ tsp. salt
1 cup unsalted butter, well
    chilled
½ cup ice water

Filling:
2 cups cranberries,
    coarsely chopped in
    food processor
1 apple peeled, cored,
    finely chopped in food
    processor
¼ cup all-purpose flour
¼ cup currants
¼ cup granulated sugar
2 tsp. melted unsalted
    butter

Glaze:
1 cup apricot jam

Make pâte brisée (tart dough):
Put the flour, sugar, and salt in the bowl of a food processor with metal blade. Cut the butter into small pieces and add it to the bowl. Pulse the mixture until the butter is completely combined with the flour. With the food processor running slowly pour in the ice water. The mixture should just come together—you don't want it to be sticky. Crumbly is fine. Turn dough out on a floured surface and pull the dough together with your hands to form a ball. If it seems too dry, sprinkle a few drops of water directly on the dough. Wrap the dough in plastic wrap and refrigerate for at least 2 hours. Take the dough out of the refrigerator and divide it into 4 pieces. Each piece will fill an 8-inch tart shell. (Freeze or refrigerate other pieces of dough for another time.) Flour the work surface. Form the dough into a ball with your hands and place the ball of dough on the floured work surface and press it down. Lightly flour the top of the dough. Use a long, thin, tapered rolling pin. Put your rolling pin down in the middle of the dough and start rolling away from you. Turn the dough slightly in a clockwise direction and roll again. Keep doing this until you have a circle about 10 inches in diameter. Place the dough on top of the tart shell. With the heel of your hand remove the excess dough. It is now ready to fill.

Continued on next page

Make filling:

Preheat oven to 350°F. Place all ingredients in a large bowl and toss to combine. Allow to sit for about 15 minutes to release the juices. Put the mixture in a fine strainer and press the fruit to remove as much liquid as possible. Then place in the prepared 8-inch tart shell lined with pastry. The cranberry mixture should completely fill the tart shell. Press it down; it can be slightly mounded. Place in oven and bake for 45 to 50 minutes. It is very hard to tell when this tart is done. It should look darker and drier than before it was baked and the edges of the tart shell should be brown. Allow to cool.

Make glaze:

Put apricot jam in a small saucepan. Place over medium heat and stir until jam becomes liquified. Remove tart from outer ring of tart shell. Place tart on serving plate with its metal bottom (a way to prevent disasters). With a pastry brush, carefully but generously apply the apricot jam to the top of the tart. Let cool. This tart will stay fresh in the refrigerator for up to 4 days.

GRANOLA

▪▪▪

I am grateful to my employee Carol Alvino Jolley for this recipe. I wanted to add granola cookies to our list and began by buying prepared granola. This didn't make sense when I had all the ingredients needed in the bakery, so Carol and I created our own homemade granola. The dried raisins and cranberries must be added after baking or they will get very hard.

MAKES 8 CUPS GRANOLA

6½ cups quick oats
½ cup brown sugar
½ cup unsalted butter, melted
¾ cup sliced almonds

½ cup honey
1 tbsp. cinnamon
½ cup raisins or dried cranberries

Preheat oven to 350°F. Combine all ingredients except raisins or cranberries in large bowl. Toss ingredients until combined. Put on cookie sheet and bake for 10 minutes. Remove pan from oven and toss mixture around with spoon. Return to oven and bake 10 to 15 minutes longer or until granola mix is browned. Allow to cool. Add raisins or cranberries and store in airtight container. Keeps up to 1 month.

BANANA RASPBERRY LOAF

This is the most popular loaf I make—and I have made thousands of them. I created this wonderful loaf for my friend Claudio Martins who worked for a NYC-based food shop called Mangia. One day he said my banana loaf is delicious, but if I added raspberries it would be out of this world. We've been putting raspberries in ever since. You're in my heart Claudio, thanks.

MAKES 8–10 SLICES

3 cups all-purpose flour

4 tsp. baking soda

½ tsp. salt

3 ripe bananas

2 cups granulated sugar

½ cup + 6 tbsp. canola oil

½ cup + 6 tbsp. buttermilk

1 tsp. pure vanilla extract

1½ cups frozen raspberries

Preheat oven to 350°F. Spray a 9-inch loaf pan and line the bottom with parchment. Measure flour, baking soda, and salt in a bowl. Mash bananas in a food processor using the metal blade. Place the bananas, sugar, oil, buttermilk, and vanilla in the bowl of an electric mixer. Beat until well combined. Add the dry ingredients, beating on low speed until incorporated. Add raspberries and beat the batter for 5 minutes on medium speed. (Don't worry if the batter is the color of gray cement.) Pour batter in prepared pan and place in the oven. Bake for 60 to 65 minutes or until the top is brown and a cake tester or long, thin knife comes out clean. Store in an airtight container. This is a very moist loaf and will keep for 1 week if well wrapped.

LEMON POPPY SEED LOAF

Some clever person put lemon rind and poppy seeds together in a cake. This is my version—lots of lemon rind and lemon juice, plus a sugar glaze. This is a delicious, moist cake. Perfect for high (or low) tea.

MAKES 12–14 SERVINGS

Loaf:
5 extra-large eggs
5 tbsp. milk
¾ tsp. pure vanilla extract
2½ cups all-purpose flour
1¼ cups granulated sugar
1¼ tsp. baking powder
¼ tsp. salt
1½ cups unsalted butter at room
   temperature
1 tbsp. lemon rind
¼ cup poppy seeds

Glaze:
½ cup lemon juice
½ cup granulated sugar

Make loaf:
Preheat oven to 350°F. Spray a 10-inch Bundt pan or 9-inch loaf pan. Put the eggs, milk, and vanilla in a bowl. In the bowl of an electric mixer, add the flour, sugar, baking powder, and salt. Cut the butter into small pieces and add it to the mixer, beating at low speed. Then add lemon rind and poppy seeds. When all the butter is incorporated, slowly add the eggs, milk, and vanilla. Beat on medium speed until the mixture becomes light, about 5 minutes. Scrape down the bowl once or twice. Fill prepared pan and place in oven. Bake for 50 to 55 minutes or until top is lightly brown and a cake tester or long, thin knife inserted comes out clean.

Make glaze:
While the loaf is baking, place the ingredients for the glaze in a microwave-safe bowl and place in the microwave for 30 seconds to dissolve the sugar. You can also make the glaze in a small saucepan on the stove over low heat, stirring until the sugar is dissolved. Allow the cake to cool, turn it out onto a flat serving plate and prick the top with a fork to allow more of the glaze to soak in. Brush the lemon glaze liberally over the top of the cake. The cake keeps up to 5 days wrapped in plastic.

CRANBERRY WALNUT LOAF

▪▪

This is a very good way to take advantage of cranberries when they are available. This loaf also works well as breakfast bread because it is not too sweet.

MAKES 10–12 SLICES

Loaf:
¾ cup unsalted butter at room temperature
1½ cups granulated sugar
4 extra-large eggs
3 cups all-purpose flour
1 tbsp. baking powder
½ tsp. baking soda
½ tsp. salt
1 cup sour cream
2 cups fresh cranberries, strained of their
    juice, chopped
1 cup chopped walnuts

Crumb topping:
¼ cup granulated sugar
¼ cup all-purpose flour
½ cup walnuts
¼ tsp. cinnamon
4 tbsp. unsalted butter, chilled

Make loaf:
Preheat oven to 350°F. Spray a 9-inch loaf pan. In the bowl of an electric mixer beat the butter and sugar until well combined. Break the eggs in a cup and add them to the mixer and beat until combined. Measure flour, baking powder, baking soda, and salt in a bowl and add to the mixer. Beat on low speed, then add the sour cream and beat until all ingredients are well combined. Add the cranberries and walnuts and mix until just combined. Place in prepared pan.

Make crumb topping:
In the bowl of the food processor place all crumb ingredients and pulse until crumbly. Sprinkle crumbs on top of loaf, place in oven, and bake for 55 to 60 minutes or until the top is firm and a cake tester or thin, long knife inserted comes out clean. Allow to cool. Loaf will keep 4 to 5 days well wrapped.

CARROT ZUCCHINI LOAF

Carrot zucchini is the second most popular loaf I make (after the banana raspberry). I am fortunate that these two ingredients are available all year round. Although there are lots of carrots and zucchini in this loaf, the first thing you will notice are the spices. If you live in New York City anywhere near Irving Farm Coffee Roasters, you can taste this carrot zucchini loaf there. It is sold in all their locations!

MAKES 10–12 SLICES

2 medium-size carrots, shredded

2 medium-size zucchinis, shredded

3 extra-large eggs

1½ cups granulated sugar

1 tsp. pure vanilla extract

1 cup canola oil

3 cups all-purpose flour

1 tbsp. baking powder

¼ tsp. cinnamon

¼ tsp. ground allspice

1 tsp. ground ginger

¼ tsp. ground nutmeg

Preheat oven to 350°F. Spray a 9-inch loaf pan. Place carrots, zucchinis, eggs, sugar, vanilla, and oil in the bowl of an electric mixer and beat to combine. In a separate bowl measure the flour, baking powder, cinnamon, allspice, ginger, and nutmeg. Add to mixer bowl and beat until all ingredients are well combined. This batter will be thick. Place in loaf pan and bake for 60 to 65 minutes or until lightly brown on top and a cake tester or long, thin knife comes out clean. Allow to cool completely. This is a very moist loaf and will keep for 1 week if well wrapped.

DOUGHNUTS

My memories of doughnut making are happy ones. There is something thrilling about the way yeast behaves in baking. The excitement is doubled when you make yeast dough that's deep fried. When you drop a yeast doughnut into hot oil it gets bigger in a second—sheer magic. The process still fills me with wonder. I once taught a group of high school students how to make doughnuts. We marveled at the process, but agreed that eating a freshly fried doughnut was even better. Deep frying doughnuts can be a cleanup nightmare—but everything else is a gratifying challenge.

MAKES 20 DOUGHNUTS

.02 ounces fresh yeast or 1 packet dry yeast

½ cup granulated sugar

½ cup milk

½ cup water

½ tsp. salt

6 tbsp. unsalted butter at room temperature

3 cups all-purpose flour

canola oil for deep frying

½ cup granulated sugar

¼ tsp. cinnamon

1 cup confectioners' sugar

¼ cup water

Place yeast, sugar, milk, water, and salt in the bowl of an electric mixer and beat on low speed. Cut butter into small pieces and add to mixer. Increase speed to medium and beat for a few minutes. Slowly add flour on low speed until it is all incorporated. If dough is not pulling away from the sides of bowl, add a little more flour. This should not be a sticky dough. Spray a large bowl. Turn dough into bowl, spraying the top and covering with plastic wrap. Let rise for 1½ hours until dough doubles in bulk. Punch the dough down and let it rise again for another 1½ to 2 hours or until dough doubles in bulk again. If the room is warm this will happen more quickly. After the second rise, you are ready to fry. Using a heavy bottomed saucepan, add canola oil about 3 inches deep. Heat oil over medium heat until a drop of water crackles when sprinkled into the oil. Place the dough on a floured work surface and lightly flour the top of the dough. With a traditional rolling pin, gently roll out the dough to ¾-inch thick. Using a doughnut cutter (or a three-inch round cutter and a smaller cutter for the center), cut the dough out and place doughnuts on a lightly floured cookie sheet. Gather remaining dough, wrap in plastic wrap, and place in the refrigerator. You can reroll this dough, but it is best to let it rest.

When oil is hot, drop as many doughnuts into the oil that fit in one layer. They will rise immediately and double in size. It is better not to crowd them; frying two at a time is fine. Have a long-handled slotted spoon ready to turn the doughnuts when they are brown; they flip easily. When both sides are

Continued on next page

brown, remove doughnuts to a paper towel–lined cookie sheet. Repeat with remaining doughnuts. Allow to cool.

Place granulated sugar and cinnamon in a small bowl and stir to combine. Roll half the doughnuts in the cinnamon sugar. Place the confectioners' sugar and water in a separate bowl and whisk until smooth, making a glaze. Dip the other half of the doughnuts in glaze by picking up each doughnut, turning it over in the glaze, and letting the excess drip off. Place doughnuts on a cookie sheet to dry. Doughnuts are best when served the day they are made.

CHAPTER SIX

191 COLUMBIA STREET

▪▪▪

RED VELVET CAKE

....

On President Street many years ago, someone asked me to make a red velvet wedding cake. The customer came from New Orleans where red velvet cake has always been popular. I said I could never make a cake that used red food coloring, and lost the order. As years went by, requests for red velvet cake increased until I finally had to give in. I learned two important lessons from this experience: If you're in business, try everything at least once—and some trends are hard to ignore. Red velvet cake is a moist, mildly chocolate cake that has a delicious cream cheese frosting between the layers.

MAKES A 1 (10-INCH) ROUND CAKE, SERVES 25 PEOPLE

Red velvet cake:
3½ cups all-purpose flour
½ cup cocoa powder
1 tsp. salt
2 cups canola oil
2¼ cups granulated sugar
3 extra-large eggs
1 tbsp. red food coloring
½ tsp. vanilla
1¼ cup buttermilk
2 tsp. baking soda
1 tbsp. distilled vinegar

Cream cheese frosting:
½ cup unsalted butter at room temperature
8 oz. cream cheese at room temperature
1 tsp. pure vanilla extract
3 cups confectioners' sugar

Make cake:

Preheat oven to 350°F. Spray 2 (10-inch) layer pans and line with parchment. Measure flour, cocoa powder, and salt in a bowl. If cocoa is lumpy, put through a sieve before putting it in the bowl. Combine canola oil, sugar, eggs, food coloring, vanilla, and buttermilk in the bowl of an electric mixer. Beat on low speed until combined. Slowly add in flour mixture and beat. Measure baking soda in small bowl and add vinegar. It will bubble up; mix with a spoon to combine and add to batter in mixer bowl. Beat until well incorporated. Pour batter into prepared pans and bake for 40 to 45 minutes or until cake is firm to the touch in the middle. Allow to cool completely.

Continued on next page

Make frosting:

Cream butter and cream cheese in bowl of electric mixer. Beat until well combined and completely smooth; scrape down bowl with rubber spatula. Add vanilla and confectioners' sugar (if confectioners' sugar is lumpy, strain through a sieve before adding to butter mixture). Beat on low speed until sugar is incorporated, increase speed, and beat until light and fluffy, about 5 minutes.

Frost the cake:

Cut out a cardboard circle the same size as cake. Remove one layer from pan, peel off parchment paper, and place on cardboard circle. Take a long serrated knife and level the top of the cake by placing the knife horizontally against the side of the cake and turning the cake as you cut. Split cake layer using the same technique. Do not remove parchment from second layer but level top and split layer in half. Put cake trimmings in food processor with metal blade. **Separate all**

four layers. With an offset spatula spread ½-inch cream cheese frosting on bottom layer and top with next layer. Repeat with next two layers. Peel parchment paper off top layer. Place cake in freezer for 1 hour to harden. Place cake on turntable and with an offset spatula frost sides of cake first and then the top. Chop cake trimmings in food processor and turn out on sheet of wax paper. With cake in your left hand (if you are right handed) grab a handful of crumbs. Press crumbs into side of cake with your right hand, turning cake after each crumb application. When you have covered the cake with crumbs, place on serving plate.

FLOURLESS CHOCOLATE CAKE

This is another surefire cake recipe. It tastes great, is gluten free, Passover appropriate, and easy to make. Alice Medrich, one of the country's foremost experts on chocolate and chocolate desserts, inspired this recipe. I recommend serving this cake with raspberries and whipped cream. It is also tasty if you add some finely chopped ancho chilies.

MAKES 12–14 SLICES

1 pound semi-sweet chocolate
1 cup unsalted butter
8 extra-large eggs

Preheat oven to 350°F. Spray an 8-inch layer pan and cut a parchment round to fit in the bottom. Put chocolate and butter in a metal bowl and place in oven to melt. After 5 minutes remove bowl from oven and stir. Return bowl to oven for another 5 minutes. Continue this until butter and chocolate are completely melted. Place eggs in the bowl of an electric mixer and beat on medium speed. Add the melted chocolate to egg mixture. Beat all ingredients until well combined, then scrape down sides of bowl with a rubber spatula. Pour mixture into prepared pan. This cake is baked in a bain-marie or water bath, meaning that your prepared pan with cake mixture must be placed into a larger pan of the same depth. Fill the larger pan with water halfway up the side of the cake pan and place in the oven. Bake for 25 to 30 minutes. When done, the top should be shiny and firm to the touch. If the cake has risen, it is overbaked. This cake can afford to be slightly underdone. Allow to cool completely. This cake keeps for 4 to 5 days well wrapped.

CHOCOLATE BABKA

▪▪▪

My grandma used to make a fantastic yeast coffee cake. Unfortunately, she never shared her best yeast dough recipes, so I have spent a lot of my career perfecting my recipe and trying to unlock the secret of her outstanding cake. It wasn't only her ingredients (although I do remember her using sour cream in place of milk), but the gentle way she handled the dough. Her arms were not strong so she only rolled small pieces of dough at a time and didn't stretch them. This is the secret to a soft, moist yeast coffee cake. It takes time, patience, and practice to achieve. It is a big challenge for the professional baker when production forces you to make big batches and give up being gentle.

MAKES 12–15 SERVINGS

Dough:

.02 ounces fresh yeast or 1 packet dry yeast

¼ cup water

½ cup granulated sugar

5 extra-large eggs

1¼ cups unsalted butter at room temperature

3 cups all-purpose flour

½ tsp. salt

Chocolate filling:

¾ cup brown sugar

1½ cups mini semi-sweet chocolate chips

4 tbsp. cocoa powder

1 cup chopped pecans

½ cup unsalted butter melted

2 extra-large eggs beaten

Make dough:

Place yeast, water, sugar, eggs, and butter in the bowl of an electric mixer and beat to combine. Add the flour and salt and mix until the flour is completely incorporated and you have a stiff but sticky dough. Remove dough and place in a large bowl that you have sprayed with pan spray. Cover with plastic wrap and place in the refrigerator for 24 hours.

Make filling:

Put all filling ingredients in a bowl and toss to combine. Set aside. Spray a 10-inch Bundt pan and line a cookie sheet with parchment. Take the dough out of the refrigerator and divide into three equal pieces. Put two pieces back in the refrigerator while you roll one. Flour a surface and roll the dough into a 9 x 12-inch rectangle. With a pastry brush, brush dough generously with melted butter and sprinkle with ⅓ of the chocolate filling. Spread to within ½-inch of the edges. Starting at the long end, roll the dough into a tight roll and place on prepared cookie sheet and refrigerate. Do the same thing with the other two pieces of dough. Place all three rolls on your work surface and gently braid them together and bring the ends together. Carefully lift the braid into the prepared Bundt pan. Brush the top with beaten egg and cover with plastic wrap and let rise for 30 minutes. Preheat oven to 350°F. Place pan in the oven, making sure it has room to rise. Bake for 1 hour to 75 minutes. It should be well browned on top and feel firm to the touch. Allow to cool completely. Babka will last up to 3 days well wrapped.

RICE CEREAL BAR

The first person to share my baking space was Kim Ima, owner of one of the first food trucks in New York, The Treats Truck. Kim took rice cereal treats to new heights. I think of her delicious version with cranberries and almonds and sunflower seeds when I make this plainer version. I never thought cereal bars would be so popular, but they're always in demand.

MAKES 9 SQUARES

4 tbsp. unsalted butter
1 (10 oz.) bag marshmallows
6 cups rice cereal

Spray a 9 x 6 x 3-inch pan. Place butter and marshmallows in a saucepan over medium heat and stir until the butter is melted and marshmallows are melted and smooth. Measure cereal into a large bowl and pour the butter and marshmallow mixture over it and gently stir the mixture with a rubber spatula until the mixture is well combined. Place the mixture into the pan and press it down with a rubber spatula to make it one even layer. Cut into squares.

WHITE CHOCOLATE CHIP BROWNIES

■▪▪

This is a very, very rich brownie. It is fudgy and creamy and gooey— all the essential qualities for a good brownie. Putting white chocolate chips on top is the fun part; you're making polka dot brownies!

MAKES 12 BROWNIES

1 pound semi-sweet chocolate

2 cups unsalted butter

2 cups granulated sugar

2 cups brown sugar

8 extra-large eggs

1½ tsp. pure vanilla extract

2 cups all-purpose flour

¾ tsp. salt

1 cup white chocolate chips, divided in half

Preheat oven to 350°F. Spray a 9 x 12 x 3-inch pan. Place chocolate and butter in a metal bowl and put in oven. Stir every 5 minutes until chocolate and butter are completely melted. Place granulated sugar, brown sugar, eggs, and vanilla in the bowl of an electric mixer. Beat until well combined. Add melted chocolate and mix on low speed. Add flour, salt, and ½ cup of white chips, (place other ½ cup in freezer until ready to use). Mix until ingredients are just combined. Pour in prepared pan and bake for 50 to 55 minutes or until top of brownie has risen and is firm to the touch. Remove from oven. While brownie is still warm, place frozen chips on top by pressing pointed side of chip into surface of brownie. Place chips randomly or in rows. You may have more chips than you need. Allow to cool. Brownies keep for 1 week well wrapped.

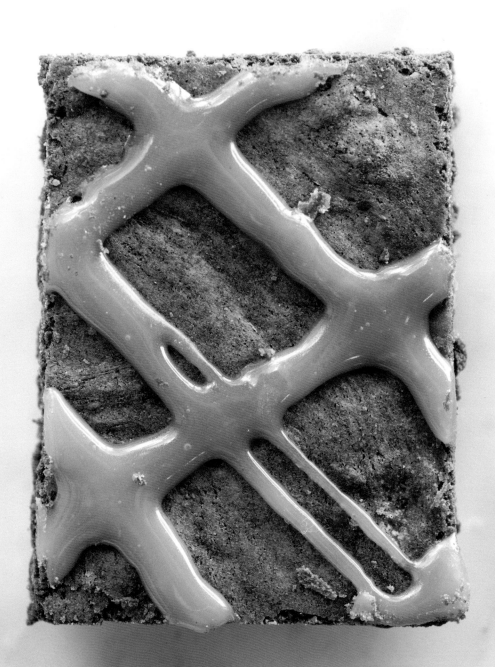

SALTED CARAMEL BROWNIES

Salt and caramel are a recent taste combo and deserve attention. Bake these brownies with fleur de sel, the delicious coarse salt from France, and you'll have a first-class treat.

MAKES 12 BROWNIES

Caramel sauce:

1¾ cups granulated sugar
1 cup water
1¾ cups heavy cream
1 cup light corn syrup
1 tsp. pure vanilla extract
2 tsp. fleur de sel or kosher salt
candy thermometer

Brownies:

5 ounces semi-sweet chocolate
5 ounces unsweetened chocolate
1 cup unsalted butter
4 extra-large eggs
1 cup brown sugar
1 cup granulated sugar
¾ tsp. pure vanilla extract
1¼ cups all-purpose flour
¾ tsp. baking powder
pinch of salt
¼ cup chopped walnuts

Make caramel sauce:

Place granulated sugar and water in heavy bottomed saucepan. Place over medium heat and allow to cook. Measure heavy cream, corn syrup, vanilla, and salt in bowl and set aside. Continue cooking sugar and water until it begins to brown. Add in cream mixture, place candy thermometer in mixture, and cook until thermometer reads 250°F. This will take about 30 minutes. Remove saucepan from heat.

Make brownies:

Preheat oven to 350°F. Spray a 12 x 9 x 3-inch pan. Place chocolates and butter in a metal bowl and place in oven to melt. Stir chocolate every 4 to 5 minutes until completely melted. Place eggs, sugars, and vanilla in the bowl of an electric mixer and beat until well combined. Add melted chocolate and beat. Measure flour, baking powder, and salt in bowl and add to mixer, beating on low speed until combined. Scoop out 3 cups of batter, place in the metal bowl used for melted chocolate, and set aside. Add walnuts to remaining batter and pour mixture in prepared pan. Spread batter to form one even layer. Pour almost all caramel sauce over brownie layer, saving ⅓ cup for decorating the top. (Put reserved caramel in a plastic container—you may need to reheat it in microwave.) Pour 3 cups of reserved brownie batter on top of caramel and cover as much of the caramel layer as possible. With an offset spatula complete the spreading. Place in oven and bake for 50 to 55 minutes or until top of the brownie is firm to touch. Allow to cool. Put reserved caramel in a 12-inch pastry bag with a large writing tip and drizzle over top of brownies in a decorative pattern. Allow to cool. Store brownies in the refrigerator for 1 week.

S'MORES BROWNIES

▪▪

This is a summertime backyard barbeque brownie. The lowly graham cracker sandwich rises to new heights with this brownie: a graham cracker crumb layer on the bottom followed by a brownie layer, a marshmallow layer, and another brownie layer. It's s'mores without the charcoal.

MAKES 12 BROWNIES

Crust:
1½ cups graham cracker
    crumbs
4 tbsp. melted unsalted
    butter

Brownies:
5 oz. semi-sweet chocolate
5 oz. unsweetened
    chocolate
1 cup unsalted butter
4 extra-large eggs
1 cup brown sugar
1 cup granulated sugar
¾ tsp. pure vanilla extract

1¼ cups all-purpose flour
¾ tsp. baking powder
¼ tsp. salt
¼ cup chopped walnuts
1 (10 oz.) package mini
    marshmallows
2 tbsp. unsalted butter
¼ cup mini chocolate chips

Make crust:
Preheat oven to 350°F. Spray a 12 x 9 x 3-inch baking pan. Place graham cracker crumbs and 4 tablespoons of melted butter in bowl and toss to mix. Press mixture in bottom of prepared pan to make one even layer. Set aside.

Make brownies:
Put chocolates and butter in metal bowl and place in oven to melt. Stir every 5 minutes until completely melted. Beat eggs, brown sugar, sugar, and vanilla in the bowl of an electric mixer. Add melted chocolate and mix well. Measure flour, baking powder, and salt in bowl and add to mixer. Stir on low speed until flour is completely incorporated. Scoop out 3 cups of batter and set aside in bowl you used to melt chocolate. Pour remaining batter over graham cracker crust in prepared pan and spread evenly. Place half the bag of mini marshmallows in saucepan with butter and stir over medium heat until marshmallows are melted. Pour marshmallow mixture over brownie layer in pan and spread evenly. It will be a thin layer. Pour reserved batter over marshmallow layer, covering marshmallow layer as best you can. Use offset spatula to spread evenly. Spread other half of mini marshmallows on top of brownie layer and sprinkle mini chocolate chips all around. Place in oven and bake 50 to 55 minutes or until marshmallows are toasted. Allow to cool. Cut with a thin, sharp knife. It will be sticky.

COCONUT LIME BARS

I like to find recipe inspiration by reading about baking around the country. This recipe was inspired by a national monthly trade publication called Bake. I usually make squares, but I suggest you make it in a 9-inch springform pan and serve it as a cake. It will be impressive.

MAKES 14–16 SERVINGS

Crust:
1 cup unsalted butter at room temperature
½ cup confectioners' sugar
2 cups all-purpose flour
½ cup toasted coconut

Filling:
12 ounces white chocolate
1½ cups heavy cream
1 lime, grated
1 cup lime juice
2½ cans sweetened condensed milk
10 extra-large egg yolks
½ cup toasted coconut

Make crust:
Preheat oven to 350°F. Spray a 9-inch springform pan and line with parchment. Beat butter, confectioners' sugar, flour, and coconut in the bowl of an electric mixer until combined and forms a ball. Press dough in prepared pan making one even layer. Place in oven and bake for 12 to 15 minutes or until lightly brown.

Make filling:
Put white chocolate and heavy cream in metal bowl and melt in oven. Stir every 5 minutes until melted. (White chocolate burns very easily.) Put melted white chocolate mixture, grated lime rind, lime juice, condensed milk, and egg yolks in bowl of electric mixer and beat until well combined. Pour over crust and bake for 15 to 20 minutes or until top is just set. Allow to cool. Chill for 1 hour in the refrigerator before cutting. Keep bars well wrapped for 4 days.

BAKED OATMEAL BARS

This is the newest recipe in my repertoire, but it has had some major repercussions. Three years ago, Cantine Catering shared my kitchen. The owner Alex Sagol and I hit it off from day one. Her business is concerned with special dietary needs and her baked oatmeal bars in particular catered to a gluten-free diet. I thought, what a wonderful way to use those dried fruits left over from Christmas baskets! I asked Alex for her blessing and developed my own version of her baked oatmeal bars to resounding success. Many customers were looking for something like this, and it has outsold many of my old staples. Another reason to be grateful for this recipe happened when a literary agent ordered a baked oatmeal bar from one of my customers. She was so excited by its taste that she tracked me down to ask if I would be interested in writing a cookbook! I was, and she arranged for this book to be published. Much gratitude to my dear Alex and to my literary agent Carla Glasser.

MAKES 6 (3-INCH) SQUARES

2 cups ambrosia*

6 cups quick oats

2 cups brown sugar

1 tbsp. baking powder

1 tsp. baking soda

½ tsp. salt

½ tsp. cinnamon

4 extra-large eggs

1 cup melted butter

2 cups milk

Preheat oven to 350°F. Spray a 6 x 9 x 3-inch baking pan. Coarsely chop ambrosia and place it in the bowl of an electric mixer. Then add all the other ingredients and mix on low speed until everything is combined. Pour into prepared pan and bake for 20 to 30 minutes or until top is lightly browned and bars are firm to the touch. Allow to cool and cut into squares. Store in an airtight container. Bars will keep for up to 4 days.

---

* The mix of dried fruits and nuts I use is available at Sahadi's on Atlantic Avenue in Brooklyn. It is a combination of almonds, cashews, walnuts, papaya, dried pineapple, apricots, and raisins.

PEANUT BUTTER BARS

Cookie cookbooks can be an inspiration. These peanut butter bars were inspired by a combination of recipes I found in a cookie cookbook. The sweetened condensed milk mixed with peanut butter makes a deliciously creamy layer sandwiched between an oat bottom and a crumbly topping of chocolate chips and chopped peanuts. Reese's, step aside!

MAKES 9 BARS

1½ (12 oz.) cans sweetened condensed milk

½ cup creamy peanut butter

3 cups quick oats

2 cups brown sugar

2¼ cups all-purpose flour

1½ tsp. baking powder

1½ cups unsalted butter, chilled

¾ tsp. baking soda

1 extra-large egg

1½ cups mini chocolate chips

1½ cups chocolate chips

¾ cup unsalted peanuts, chopped

Preheat oven to 350°F. Spray a 12 x 9 x 3-inch baking pan. Put sweetened condensed milk in small bowl and add peanut butter. Stir peanut butter into condensed milk until mixture is smooth. Set aside. In bowl of electric mixer combine oats, brown sugar, flour, and baking powder. Mix on low speed to combine. Cut butter into small pieces and add to mixer bowl. Beat until butter is completely incorporated. Mixture will be crumbly. Remove ½ of mixture and place in large bowl. Set aside. Add baking soda and egg to what is left in mixer bowl and beat until combined. Put mixture in prepared pan and smooth down to form an even layer. Place pan in oven and bake for 10 to 12 minutes or until bottom is evenly browned. While bottom is baking add both kinds of chocolate chips and peanuts to the other half of mixture. Toss until everything is well distributed and set aside. Remove pan from oven. Pour condensed milk mixture evenly over bottom crust and cover with chocolate chip and peanut mixture. The pan will be full but these bars do not rise. Return pan to oven and bake for another 20 to 25 minutes. The top should be lightly brown and set. Do not touch top because the chocolate chips will be soft and very hot. Allow to cool completely and refrigerate before cutting. Stored in an airtight container in the refrigerator. Bars will keep for 1 week.

PUMPKIN CHEESECAKE BARS

▀▄

A seasonal bar is something to look forward to, and these bars have a large following. As soon as summer is over, everyone begins to ask for pumpkin bars. Pumpkin and cream cheese go very well together—pumpkin makes the cream cheese even creamier.

MAKES 18 BARS

Crust:
2 cups all-purpose flour
1½ tsp. baking soda
¼ tsp. salt
1 tsp. cinnamon
1 extra-large egg
¾ cup white sugar
¾ cup brown sugar
6 tbsp. canola oil
1 (15 oz.) can pumpkin purée

Filling:
1½ pounds cream cheese
1 cup brown sugar
1⅓ cups granulated sugar
1 (15 oz.) can pumpkin purée
6 extra-large eggs
1 tbsp. flour
1 tsp. ginger
1 tsp. nutmeg
1½ tsp. cinnamon

Make crust:
Preheat oven to 350°F. Spray a 9 x 12 x 3-inch pan. Measure flour, baking soda, salt, and cinnamon in bowl. Beat egg and sugars in the bowl of an electric mixer, add oil and pumpkin purée and beat until combined. Add flour mixture slowly and beat until well combined. Spread 1-inch thick batter evenly in bottom of prepared pan. Set aside.

Make filling:
Place cream cheese in bowl of electric mixer and beat until smooth. Add sugars and beat until well combined. Add pumpkin purée. Break eggs into a separate bowl and add them to the mixer. Measure flour, ginger, nutmeg, and cinnamon in a small bowl and add to mixer. Beat on medium speed for 5 to 7 minutes, scraping down sides of bowl with rubber spatula. Pour this mixture over batter in prepared pan and place in oven. Bake 55 to 60 minutes or until center is set and firm to the touch. Allow to cool. These bars will keep up to 1 week in the refrigerator.

CREAM CHEESE BERRY BARS

How do you make cheesecake in individual portions that can be displayed in a pastry case and sold in a bag to be eaten on the go? These were the challenges I faced with this bar. A graham cracker crust was a logical bottom for cheesecake, but I didn't want to go the easy route, so I experimented with a shortbread bottom, a creamy cheesecake layer with berries folded in, and dots of raspberry jam for decoration. Not only had I met the challenge, but the cheesecake didn't crack in the middle! I call it successful and tasty problem solving.

MAKES 9 BARS

Crust:

1 cup unsalted butter at room temperature

½ cup confectioners' sugar

2 cups all-purpose flour

Filling:

3 (8-ounce) packages cream cheese

2 cups granulated sugar

2 tbsp. all-purpose flour

6 extra-large eggs

¾ cup frozen raspberries

1 cup frozen blueberries

½ cup raspberry preserves

Make crust:

Preheat oven to 350°F. Spray a 12 x 9 x 3-inch pan. Beat butter, confectioners' sugar, and flour in the bowl of an electric mixer until it is combined and forms a ball. Press the dough in the prepared pan making one even layer. Place in oven and bake for 12 to 15 minutes or until it is lightly brown.

Make filling:

While the crust is baking, beat cream cheese with sugar and flour in bowl of electric mixer until well combined and very smooth. Break eggs into a cup and add them to the mixer and continue to beat on medium speed for 7 to 10 minutes. Remove bowl from the mixer and add raspberries and blueberries, folding them in with a rubber spatula. Pour mixture into the pan on top of the crust and return to oven for 45 to 50 minutes or until center is firm to the touch and top is lightly brown. Allow to cool completely. It will be easier to cut if you refrigerate the bars for 2 hours. Cut the bars into squares using a long, thin, sharp knife. Heat the knife by running it under hot water if you having trouble cutting neatly. Place raspberry jam in a 12-inch pastry bag with coupler and pipe a small amount of jam on each square. You can also spoon the jam on each square with a teaspoon. Bars can be stored in the refrigerator for up to 1 week.

PECAN BARS

▪▪

I like these bars almost better than my pecan tarts. The crust is shorter and sweeter than pie dough. I invented these bars because I knew they would sell well at Thanksgiving time and look beautiful in a display case.

MAKES 9 BARS

Crust:
1 cup unsalted butter at room temperature
½ cup confectioners' sugar
2 cups all-purpose flour

Filling:
6 extra-large eggs
2 cups dark corn syrup
1 cup granulated sugar
4 tbsp. butter, melted
2 tsp. pure vanilla extract
3 cups pecan halves

Make crust:
Preheat oven to 350°F. Spray 12 x 9 x 3-inch pan. Beat butter, confectioners' sugar, and flour in the bowl of an electric mixer until it is combined and forms a ball. Press dough in prepared pan, making one even layer. Place in oven and bake for 12 to 15 minutes or until lightly brown.

Make filling:
In a large bowl beat eggs, corn syrup, sugar, melted butter, and vanilla with whisk until everything is well combined. Sprinkle pecan halves on baked pastry and then pour egg mixture on top. Carefully place in oven and bake for 45 to 50 minutes or until mixture has risen slightly and is firm to the touch. Allow to cool. Bars keep up to 1 week in an airtight container.

FAMOUS CANDY COOKIES

Cookies with candy on them are sure to please the kids. Throw some M&M's in the dough and save some for the top— and some to nibble on until the cookies are done.

MAKES 24–30 (3-INCH) COOKIES

1 cup unsalted butter at room temperature
¾ cup granulated sugar
¾ cup brown sugar
2 extra-large eggs
½ tsp. pure vanilla extract

2 cups all-purpose flour
1 tsp. baking soda
¼ tsp. salt
2 cups M&M's

Preheat oven to 350°F. Spray a 10 x 15-inch cookie sheet with pan spray or line with parchment. In the bowl of an electric mixer beat butter and sugars until well combined. Break eggs in a cup and add them with the vanilla and beat until combined. Measure the flour, baking soda, and salt in a bowl and add to the mixer, beating on low speed. When all the flour is incorporated add 1½ cups of M&M's to the batter. Form the dough into balls the size of ping pong balls. Eight should fit on the cookie sheet and give the cookies room to spread. Bake 12 to 15 minutes or until very lightly browned. Remove from oven and while cookies are still warm press 4 to 5 M&M's into each cookie. Allow to cool. Bake all of the dough or place in a plastic container. It will last in the refrigerator for up to 2 weeks or 3 months in the freezer.

WHOOPEE PIES

▪▪

"When in south Brooklyn, we like to swing by the Red Hook Lobster Pound, not just for Connecticut-style lobster rolls, but to grab one of Margaret Palca Bakes's spectacular whoopee pies." —New York magazine

Enough said!

MAKES 12 WHOOPEE PIES

Whoopee pies:
2 cups flour
½ cup cocoa powder
1¼ tsp. baking soda
½ tsp. salt
1 extra-large egg
1 cup sugar
1 tsp. pure vanilla extract
½ cup canola oil
1 cup buttermilk

Filling:
4 tbsp. unsalted butter at room
    temperature
½ cup marshmallow fluff
¼ tsp. pure vanilla extract
⅓ cup confectioners' sugar

Make whoopee pies:
Preheat oven to 350°F. Line 3 (10 x 15-inch) cookie sheets with parchment or spray. Measure flour, cocoa, baking soda, and salt in bowl. Combine egg and sugar in the bowl of an electric mixer Add vanilla, oil, and buttermilk and beat until well blended. Add in flour mixture and beat on low speed until all ingredients are incorporated. Fill a 12-inch pastry bag with coupler half-full with batter. Pipe a two-inch round of batter on cookie sheet. Repeat this process eight times on each cookie sheet; they should be ½-inch apart. Bake for 12 to 14 minutes or until whoopees are firm to the touch. Allow to cool.

Make filling:
Put filling ingredients in bowl of electric mixer and beat until light and spreadable consistency. Turn half of the whoopee pies over. Fill a 12-inch pastry bag with coupler with filling and pipe filling over entire surface of pie. Top with remaining whoopie pie. Repeat with all whoopee pies. Whoopee pies keep for up to 4 days well wrapped.

VEGAN MAPLE PECAN COOKIES

This is a delicious vegan oatmeal cookie. In my opinion, the best vegan recipes are ones where dietary restrictions are invisible. That's certainly true of this cookie. Nothing is missing except dairy products—and it's almost impossible to know (or taste) the difference!

MAKES 24 COOKIES

3 cups quick oats

1 cup sweetened flaked coconut

2⅔ cups all-purpose flour

1 tsp. salt

1 tsp. cinnamon

2 tsp. baking soda

2 cups brown sugar

1 cup canola oil

½ cup maple syrup

2 tbsp. light corn syrup

¼ cup water

1 tsp. pure vanilla extract

2 cups chopped pecans

24 pecan halves to decorate tops of cookies

Preheat oven to 350°F. Spray a 10 x 15-inch cookie sheet or line with parchment. Measure oats, coconut, flour, salt, cinnamon, and baking soda in a bowl and set aside. Combine brown sugar, canola oil, maple syrup, corn syrup, water, and vanilla in the bowl of an electric mixer and beat on low speed. Add in oat mixture to mixer, beating on low speed until everything is well mixed. Add chopped pecans and beat to combine. Form dough into balls the size of ping pong balls. Press balls down slightly with palm of your hand and place 1 pecan half on top of each. Eight should fit on the cookie sheet and give the cookies room to spread. Bake 12 to 15 minutes or until cookies are firm and lightly brown. Allow to cool. Cookies can be stored in an airtight container for up to 1 week.

CHOCOLATE FUDGE CHIP COOKIES

One day I rode my bicycle to Dumbo in Brooklyn to buy a baguette from a small French pastry shop. Jacques Torres Chocolate shop was across the street and I decided to go in. I saw some chocolate chip cookies in a basket that looked quite special with huge chunks of chocolate and fudge swirled throughout the batter. I couldn't wait to get back to my kitchen and try to make my own version of that cookie. It was the birth of my chocolate fudge chip cookie. A bit more trouble to make than its brother, the traditional chocolate chip cookie, but well worth the effort.

MAKES 24–30 COOKIES

Dough:
1 cup + 8 tbsp. unsalted butter at room temperature
¾ cup granulated sugar
¾ cup brown sugar
2 extra-large eggs
½ tsp. pure vanilla extract
2 cups all-purpose flour

1 tsp. baking soda
¼ tsp. salt
1 pound semi-sweet chocolate
¾ cup dark corn syrup
½ cup water
1 cup semi-sweet chocolate chips

Glaze:
½ pound semi-sweet chocolate
6 tbsp. dark corn syrup
¼ cup water
4 tbsp. butter

In the bowl of an electric mixer beat 1 cup butter and sugars until well combined. Break eggs in a cup and add them to the mixer bowl with the vanilla and beat until combined. Measure the flour, baking soda, and salt in a bowl and add it to the mixer. Beat on low speed until flour is incorporated. Line a cookie sheet with parchment paper and spread the dough in one even layer.

Put semi-sweet chocolate, corn syrup, water, and remaining butter in large metal bowl and place in oven until melted. Stir chocolate glaze every 5 minutes for 15 to 20 minutes until completely melted and pour over the dough, spreading it ½ inch of the edges. Place dough in refrigerator and chill for at least 2 hours. Preheat oven to 350°F. Spray a 10 x 15-inch cookie sheet or line with parchment paper. Place chocolate chips in a shallow bowl. Remove the dough on the cookie sheet from the refrigerator. Bring the outside edges of the dough together to cover the chocolate. Then break off pieces of dough the size of ping pong balls, making sure the dough surrounds the chocolate. Roll the balls of dough into the chocolate chips and place on the cookie sheet. Eight should fit on the cookie sheet and give the cookies room to spread. Bake 12 to 15 minutes or until very lightly browned. Repeat with remaining dough or place in the refrigerator in a plastic container. The dough will keep for up to 2 weeks in the refrigerator or in the freezer for up to 3 months.

GLUTEN-FREE PEANUT BUTTER CHIP COOKIES

These cookies are thanks to my daughter Julie. About twelve years ago she went to college in North Carolina and many of her friends were on gluten-free diets. How could I send her a care package of cookies she could share with her friends? What could I make without flour—the basis of all my baking? I came up with this recipe. I prefer not using flour at all rather than finding a flour substitute. You don't have to be on a gluten-free diet to enjoy this cookie!

MAKES 12–14 (3-INCH) COOKIES

2 cups creamy peanut butter

2 cups brown sugar

2 extra-large eggs

2 tsp. baking soda

2 cups mini semi-sweet chocolate chips

Preheat oven to 350°F. Spray a 10 x 15-inch cookie sheet or line with parchment. In a bowl mix peanut butter and brown sugar. (You can use the electric mixer, but mixing by hand is easy with this recipe.) Add the eggs and baking soda and mix, then add the mini chocolate chips and stir until everything is well incorporated. Form dough into balls the size of ping pong balls. Eight should fit on the cookie sheet and give the cookies room to spread. Bake for 12 to 15 minutes until they are brown and firm on the top. Repeat with remaining dough or refrigerate the extra dough; it will keep up to 2 weeks in the refrigerator or 3 months in the freezer.

MARGARET'S ROLLS

I started bread baking about eighteen years ago when we moved to Columbia Street in Brooklyn and decided to open a cafe. The menu included sandwiches, but the bread companies all had large minimum orders and I couldn't bear to throw away so much bread every day, so I decided to make my own bread. I started by reading Nancy Silverton's Breads from the La Brea Bakery cookbook, Amy's Bread cookbook, and also took inspiration from Bernard Clayton's and James Beard's bread recipes. After much trial and error, I perfected my own bread recipe. A former employee, Joplin Steinweis, who left us to work for Amy's Bread, had agreed to give me some helpful pointers. Now we had fresh rolls every morning for breakfast and lunch sandwiches. To my good fortune, soon after I started to make bread, I hired a head baker who had worked for Cammerari, a local Brooklyn bread bakery, who took my bread production to a whole new level. He was so good at making bread that we even had challah occasionally. Armando Mendes, every time I form a roll I see your skillful hands. I'm still trying!

MAKES 7–8 ROLLS

.01 fresh yeast or ½ packet dry yeast

1½ cups water

1½ tsp. kosher salt or coarse sea salt (don't use ordinary salt)

3½ cups all-purpose flour

¼ cup fine yellow cornmeal

Place all ingredients in the bowl of an electric mixer fitted with a dough hook (most KitchenAid mixers come with a dough hook). Without a dough hook you could damage the mixer. Knead dough ingredients with the paddle for 10 minutes. Beat the mixture until it comes together. Stop the machine and allow dough to sit in the mixer bowl for 5 minutes. Then turn machine back on to medium speed and let the mixer knead the bread for 10 minutes. (Be sure to keep an eye on the mixer the whole time—the newer mixers are light and the weight of the dough can make the mixer move). After 10 minutes turn mixer off. Spray a large bowl with pan spray and place dough in the bowl. Lightly spray the top of the dough and cover it with plastic wrap and allow to rise for 1½ hours. Punch dough down, turn it over, lightly spray top again, and recover with plastic wrap. Let rise for another 1 to 1½ hours or until dough doubles in size.

Continued on next page

Line a 10 x 15-inch cookie sheet with parchment paper. Turn dough onto a floured surface. A food scale is useful at this point but not essential. Take a bench scraper and cut one long strip of dough. Make sure the surface is well floured. Bread dough sticks to itself very easily. Divide the dough into equal pieces; each piece of dough should weigh .25 on a digital scale. This is the size roll we make, an easy size for the average hand to roll. Once you have divided all the dough into equal pieces you are ready to form rolls.

Sprinkle the cookie sheet with cornmeal. Take a piece of dough and roll it into itself on the table. The piece of dough will start out limp so the goal is to make it a taut, firm ball but not sticky. Place the rolls about two inches apart on your cookie sheet. You should have between 7 and 8 rolls. Spray the tops of rolls and cover well with plastic wrap. Place the entire tray in a large plastic bag and tie the end. Place the tray in the refrigerator for at least 4 hours or up to 2 days.

Here's a baker's secret: If you want to bake bread for breakfast, take the tray out at 9 p.m. the night before and put on counter. The next morning, preheat oven to 450°F. Carefully remove the tray from the large plastic bag. Gently pull plastic wrap off the rolls. You can score the tops of the rolls by gently slashing them with a razor blade. Place rolls in oven. Bake for 6 to 10 minutes; they will be lightly brown. Do not leave the room while you are baking them as you need to keep a close eye on them. Remove from oven and allow to cool. They are best the day they are baked, but they can be frozen in an airtight plastic bag.

WHOLE WHEAT BREAD

▪▪▪

If you make white bread you must try making whole wheat. I add oats, flax seeds, and bran—you're getting fiber, grains, and unbleached flour. These ingredients not only taste good but give the bread personality.

MAKES 7–8 ROLLS

.01 fresh yeast or ½ packet dry yeast
1¼ cups cold water
¼ cup molasses
1 cup all-purpose flour
½ cup rolled oats
½ cup wheat bran

1½ cups whole wheat flour
1 tbsp. flax seeds
1½ tsp. kosher salt or coarse sea salt
1 tbsp. fine yellow cornmeal
2 tbsp. rolled oats
spray bottle filled with water

Combine yeast, water, and molasses in the bowl of an electric mixer fitted with a dough hook. You cannot make this recipe without a dough hook—it will be too taxing for your mixer. In a separate bowl measure flour, oats, bran, whole wheat flour, flax seeds, and salt. Add to mixer. Beat on low speed until all ingredients are combined and have come together in a ball. Stop machine and allow dough to rest for 5 minutes. Turn machine on again and beat on medium speed for 10 minutes. This will knead the dough. If dough sticks to sides of bowl add a small amount of flour to make it pull away from sides. After 10 minutes remove dough from machine and place in a large bowl sprayed with pan spray. Cover dough lightly with plastic wrap and let rise for 1 to 1½ hours. Punch dough down and cover with plastic wrap and let rise again for 1 more hour. It should double in bulk. Line a 10 x 15-inch cookie sheet with parchment paper and sprinkle with cornmeal. When dough has risen, turn out on floured surface. Divide dough into 7 or 8 pieces. Each piece should weigh ¼ pound when weighed on scale. Form dough into tight balls (see directions on pg. 184). Space rolls apart on cookie sheet to give them room to rise. Spray tops with pan spray and cover with plastic wrap. Place whole cookie sheet in plastic garbage bag and secure with twist tie. Put in refrigerator for 5 hours or up to two days. The night before you are ready to bake rolls, remove from refrigerator at 9 p.m. and leave on counter to rise all night.

Next morning, preheat oven to 450°F. Carefully remove garbage bag and plastic wrap. Sprinkle small amount of oats in the center of each roll and spray tops with water from spray bottle. Place rolls in middle of oven and bake for 7 to 10 minutes, watching carefully to make sure they are not burning. When done they will be lightly brown on top. Allow to cool. Whole wheat rolls can be stored in a plastic bag for up to 2 days or frozen for 1 week.

PIZZA DOUGH

We look forward to Saturday night all week long. It's homemade pizza night at our house and we never get tired of it. We use at least two kinds of olives, dry salami, roasted vegetables, our favorite Portobello mushrooms, and at least four kinds of cheeses. An old vine zinfandel goes down well, but we like to experiment. Too much pizza and wine ends our week perfectly. Here's the crust. The toppings are limited only by your imagination and taste. (Use pineapple at your own risk.)

MAKES 3 (18-INCH) PIZZAS

.04 yeast or 2 packets dry yeast

2½ cups cold water

5 cups all-purpose flour

2 tbsp. kosher salt

Place all ingredients in the bowl of an electric mixer with dough hook or paddle. Beat until dough is combined and pulling away from sides of bowl. Remove from bowl and place in bowl you have sprayed. Cover dough with plastic wrap. Refrigerate at least 2 to 4 hours or up to 2 days. Remove dough from refrigerator and divide into 3 pieces. Form pieces into tight balls, roll in flour, and cover each piece with plastic wrap. Refrigerate the balls until you are ready to use them. Allow the dough to rest for at least 4 to 5 hours before forming.

Preheat oven to 425°F. Spray an 18-inch aluminum pan. Remove dough from refrigerator and place on floured surface and sprinkle some flour on top. Stretch dough out with your hands. Then lift it up, make your hands into fists, drape the dough over them, and gently pull and stretch the dough. Keep stretching and turning until the dough is the size you want. Place in prepared pan, stretching edges of dough until it reaches the ends of the pan. You're on your own for topping. The pizza will take 20 to 25 minutes to bake. Check frequently; if the bottom is browning too quickly put it on a higher rack in the oven. Pizza dough can be frozen up to 6 months.

CRANBERRY ALMOND SCONES

■▪■

These scones are healthy and a great start to the day. This version is a far cry from its English cousin.

MAKES 6 SCONES

1 cup all-purpose flour	8 tbsp. cold unsalted butter
1 cup whole wheat flour	½ cup dried cranberries
1 cup quick oats	¼ cup raisins
1 cup sliced almonds	¼ cup pumpkin seeds
⅓ cup brown sugar	¼ cup sunflower seeds
1 tsp. baking soda	½ cup buttermilk
1 tsp. baking powder	1 beaten egg
½ tsp. salt	raw sugar for sprinkling

Preheat oven to 350°F. Line a 10 x 15-inch cookie sheet with parchment paper or spray. Place flours, oats, almonds, brown sugar, baking soda, baking powder, salt, and butter in a food processor with metal blade. Pulse until butter is completely incorporated. Put cranberries, raisins, pumpkin seeds, and sunflower seeds in large bowl and add contents from food processor. Add buttermilk and work with your hands until mixture forms a ball. You may need to add a little more buttermilk slowly until it all comes together. Remove from bowl onto lightly floured surface and form into a disc 8 inches in diameter. Cut disc in half with long knife and cut each half into thirds. Place on cookie sheet. Brush with beaten egg and sprinkle tops with raw sugar. Bake for 20 to 25 minutes or until brown on the top. Remove from oven and allow to cool. Scones are best eaten the day they are made.

BLUEBERRY OR RASPBERRY SCONES

Scones lend themselves to many variations. You can be creative, just start with the basic flour-butter-baking powder mix and then add things you like: cheddar cheese, chives, bacon, gruyere. Chocolate chips always work well. Bake scones and enjoy them immediately while they're at their best.

MAKES 6 SCONES

1 cup all-purpose flour
1 cup whole wheat flour
1 cup quick oats
1 cup sliced almonds
2 tsp. baking powder
1 tsp. salt

8 tbsp. unsalted butter, well chilled
1 cup frozen blueberries or frozen
    raspberries
½ cup milk
1 beaten egg
raw sugar for sprinkling

Preheat oven to 350°F. Line a 10 x 15-inch cookie sheet with parchment or spray. Put flours, oats, almonds, baking powder, salt, and butter cut in pieces in the bowl of a food processor with metal blade. Pulse until butter is fully incorporated. Put contents of food processor in large bowl and add berries. Slowly add milk stirring with your hands until mixture has enough liquid to form a ball. If mixture is dry, add small amounts of milk just to make dough come together. Turn out on floured surface and form into an 8-inch disc. Cut the disc in half with long knife and then cut each half into thirds. Place pieces on cookie sheet. Brush tops with beaten egg and sprinkle with raw sugar. Bake for 20 to 25 minutes or until tops are brown. Remove from oven and allow to cool. Scones are best eaten the day they are baked.

VEGAN CARROT MUFFINS

This is the latest muffin to join our menu. When we first moved to Columbia Street it was quiet until some men started to build a restaurant in the empty lot next door. These men took their needed breaks in my café and Anthony, one of the owners, always asked me to make him a carrot muffin until I finally accepted the challenge. These muffins did not start out as vegan; it happened by popular demand because this recipe lends itself to vegan requirements. There are no eggs, canola oil can be substituted for butter, and soy milk replaces the dairy. It is a moist, slightly sweet muffin—and vegan to boot. Thank you, Anthony Capone, for insisting.

MAKES 7–8 MUFFINS

2 carrots, shredded

1 cup brown sugar

½ cup canola oil

1¼ cups soy milk

2½ cups all-purpose flour

1 tbsp. baking powder

1 tsp. baking soda

¼ tsp. salt

½ tsp. cinnamon

½ cup raisins

Preheat oven to 350°F. Spray a 12-muffin (½-cup capacity) pan. Combine all ingredients in a large bowl and stir well to combine. Spoon batter into the muffin cups and fill to the top. These muffins rise a lot so don't overfill. You will get 7 to 8 muffins. Bake for 25 to 30 minutes or until lightly browned and firm to the touch. Allow to cool. Muffins taste best the day they are made but can be frozen for up to 3 months.

CHOCOLATE CHIP ICE CREAM SANDWICHES

I hope some young and mature bakers alike will look to Maida Heatter's dessert cookbooks for baking inspiration. She is the final word on baking as far as I'm concerned, and was the inspiration for this recipe. Vanilla ice cream sandwiched between two chocolate chip cookies is a really nice treat.

MAKES 12–15 CHOCOLATE CHIP ICE CREAM SANDWICHES

Chocolate chip cookies:
1 cup unsalted butter at
    room temperature
¾ cup granulated sugar
¾ cup brown sugar
2 extra-large eggs
½ tsp. pure vanilla extract

2 cups all-purpose flour
1 tsp. baking soda
¼ tsp. salt
⅓ cup chopped walnuts
2 cups semi-sweet
    chocolate chips

Vanilla ice cream:
3 cups heavy cream
6 extra-large egg yolks
¾ cup granulated sugar
½ tsp pure vanilla extract

Make cookies:
Preheat oven to 350°F. Spray a 10 x 15-inch cookie sheet or line it with parchment paper. In the bowl of an electric mixer beat the butter and sugars at medium speed until well combined. Break the eggs into a cup and add them to the mixer with the vanilla. Measure the flour, baking soda, and salt into a small bowl and add it to the mixer beating on low speed until the flour is combined. Add in walnuts and chocolate chips and mix until combined. If the dough is very soft, chill it for 30 minutes. Form the dough into balls about the size of a ping pong ball. The dough will make 24 to 30 cookies. Eight should fit on the cookie sheet and give the cookies room to spread. Bake 10 to 12 minutes or until lightly brown. Remove from oven and allow the cookies to cool. Place cookies in the freezer for at least 2 hours or overnight before making the ice cream sandwiches.

Make ice cream:
Please note an ice cream machine is required. Heat heavy cream in a saucepan over medium heat until simmering. Place egg yolks and sugar in a bowl and beat with whisk until very light in color. When cream is hot, slowly pour it into the bowl with egg yolks and sugar, beating as you pour. Return mixture to saucepan and cook, stirring constantly until mixture is thick enough to coat a spoon. Remove from heat, allow to cool, then add vanilla. Put mixture in plastic container and place in refrigerator for at least 24 hours. Put mixture in ice cream machine.

Assemble ice cream sandwiches:
Place scoop of ice cream directly from ice cream machine on frozen cookie. Cover with another cookie and put ice cream sandwich directly in freezer.

GINGERBREAD HOUSE

▪▪

My husband Paul and I met at Fraser Morris where I worked for about five years. (During that time, by the way, we got married!) What we learned and tasted there was extraordinary: spoonfuls of the finest beluga caviar, smoked salmon flown in from Scotland, fraises des bois from France, truffles from Périgord (costing eight hundred dollars a pound)! We watched a master baker make beautiful traditional German gingerbread houses with marzipan figures waving from the window. When we moved to Brooklyn, we needed to figure out how to fill orders for the gingerbread house customers we inherited because the German bakery nearby had gone out of business. I tried my best and my first attempts met with great success. My gingerbread houses are a labor of love and family participation. Paul and I, my mother (who added a licorice scotty dog to guard the house), and occasionally a reluctant daughter Katie or Julie joined in the production. We make each house the same way, but there is no right or wrong. Enjoy yourself, get very sticky, and try not to eat too many gumdrops and M&M's.

MAKES 1 GINGERBREAD HOUSE

Equipment needed:
Gingerbread house cutter
    bake set
String
Offset spatula
Small rectangular cookie
    cutter
Large rounded cookie
    cutter
Metal grater with a fine
    side
Pastry brush
Holly leaf decorations
Green and red food colors
12-inch pastry bag for
    green royal icing
12-inch pastry bag for
    white royal icing
Green sanding sugar
12-inch pastry bag for red
    royal icing

2 (12-inch) pastry bags
Couplers, tips
Sturdy cardboard bottom
    to place house on

Dough:
¾ cup vegetable
    shortening
1¼ cups brown sugar
2 extra-large eggs
1½ cups molasses
6½ cups all-purpose flour
2 tsp. baking soda
1 tsp. baking powder
2½ tsp. ginger
1½ tsp. cinnamon
½ tsp. cloves
1 tsp. salt

Royal icing:
½ cup (whites from
    approximately 8 eggs)
    egg whites
6½ cups confectioners'
    sugar

Candy suggestions:
Candy Canes
Mini Candy Canes
M&M's
Spice Gum Drops
Green Apple Gummy
    Rings
Chocolate balls (like Lindt)
Fruit Slices
Spearmint Leaves sugar-
    coated jelly candies
Peppermint mints
Licorice Scottie Dogs

Continued on next page

Make dough:

In the bowl of the electric mixer beat the shortening and brown sugar until well combined. Break eggs in a small bowl and add them to the mixer, beat until combined, then add the molasses and beat well. Measure the flour, baking soda, baking powder, ginger, cinnamon, cloves, and salt in a bowl and slowly add to the mixer bowl. Beat well after combined. Wrap dough in plastic wrap and refrigerate overnight.

Preheat oven to 350°F. Line three (10 x 15-inch) cookie sheets with parchment. Remove the dough from the refrigerator and cut off ⅓ of the dough and place remaining dough back in refrigerator. On a floured surface with a traditional rolling pin, roll the dough out to ¼-inch thick. Make sure you have flour under the dough at all times. If you find there is no flour under the dough, sprinkle some flour around the edges of the dough and with a long piece of string held taut in both hands, run the string under the dough, dragging the flour. Try to roll out the dough as evenly as possible but be sure not to let the dough get too thin.

Each house must have two sides, two roofs, one back, and one front. The gingerbread cutter bake set does not represent exactly how I make the house. There is a door on the side of one of the cutters that I always remove. Cut out as many pieces as you can. Pick the pieces of the house up with the help of a long, offset spatula and guide them to the cookie sheet with your hands. You may only get two sides on one cookie sheet.

If you have extra space and rolled dough, use small rectangle cutter in kit to make seven pieces (6 windows and a door), use one large rounded window cutter once, and then cut out one snowman and one tree. Place the already rolled dough back in the refrigerator to chill and bring out another 1/3 of the dough. When you have cut out all the sides and windows you need, place the cookie sheets in the oven and bake for 20-25 minutes or until the cookies are very firm to the touch and brown. Allow to cool.

Make icing:

There are many ways to decorate. This way works best for me. You will need a lot of equipment (refer to pg. 197). You must have more than one pastry bag, food colors, offset spatula, patience, determination, and a steady hand. Place the egg whites in the bowl of an electric mixer with the whisk attachment and beat until stiff peaks form. Change to the paddle attachment and slowly add the confectioners' sugar. Beat on slow speed until all the sugar is added. If the confectioners' sugar is lumpy put it through a sifter or strainer before adding to the egg whites. Beat the mixture well until all sugar is added. It should be as thick as whipped cream cheese. It is important to place the royal icing in a plastic container with a tight lid. Air makes royal icing dry out and crunchy spots can form.

Assemble gingerbread house:

To prepare the sides of the houses, you need to grate the edges so they will fit together smoothly and stand level on their base. With the fine side of a metal grater, even the edges by gently running them against a grater. For the roof pieces, you only need to grate one of the long sides on an angle so it will meet the other side. With a dry pastry brush, remove the cookie crumbs you have made by grating. Leave the sides of the house on the cookie sheets. Decorate the windows. Pour some of the holly decorations on a piece of wax paper. Save one of the small rectangles for the door. With the other 6 rectangles, use a green royal icing–filled pastry bag and pipe a green line at the bottom edge of the cookie and dip it into the holly decorations. Repeat with all the windows including the rounded window. With a white royal icing–filled pastry bag, outline the window cookie and make window panes. For the door, put some green sanding sugar on a piece of wax paper. Make a small circle near the top of the cookie with the green pastry bag and then turn the cookie over into the sugar. With the red royal icing–filled pastry bag, make a few dots around the green ring, make a small bow at the bottom of the ring, outline the door, and make a door knob.

Fill 2 (12-inch) pastry bags half full with royal icing. Squeeze a large dot of icing on the back of each window cookie and place it on the house. I put a jelly wreath on the top of the front of the house and a star mint on the top of the back of the house. Allow the decorations at least three hours to dry, but overnight is preferable. Now you are ready to build up the sides. Place the front and back of the house upside down on the cookie sheets. Pipe royal icing on both sides of the front of

the house and both sides of the back, from the bottom up to where it meets the roof. Stand up the front of the house and stick a side of the house into the icing. It will stand on its own. Do the same with the other side. Carefully place the back of the house to the sides. Push gently with one hand on the back of the house and one hand on the front of the house. Be sure the sides are straight up and down; move them gently if they need to be straightened. Now leave it alone. It must dry for at least 24 hours.

Twenty-four hours later you can put on the roof. Pipe icing on all four slanted sides of the house and place the roof parts down on the slanted sides, making sure the pieces meet at the top of the house. Hold the pieces together with your hands for 1 minute until you are sure it is holding. Pipe a line of icing across the top of the roof. Allow the roof to dry for 24 hours. Cover a cardboard base with aluminum foil and lift the house up and place in on the cardboard. Trace the outline of the house with a knife. Remove the house and pipe along the outline you have made. Then rest the house on the ring

Continued on next page

of royal icing. Now you are ready to complete the decorating of the house. Pipe some royal icing on any of the candies you want to stick on the house. You are now the architect. Once the decorations are all on the house it will need at least 24 hours to dry. The house will look beautiful for more than a month and the gingerbread will still taste great.

The crew, 2020

ACKNOWLEDGMENTS

This book would not be possible if not for the extremely hard work of my agent Carla Glasser and my editor extraordinaire Nicole Mele.

I have already said a lot about Grandma Wilk. She was my first inspiration.

Grandma Palca baked one kind of cookie, and although she loathed baking, it gave me a chance to bake with her.

Alfred Palca, 1920–1998

Then comes my mother and father. Although they spent a great deal of money on my education in art history, they have always been supportive of my passion for baking, from providing resources when needed, to helping me find customers and then delivering to said customers. My mother has probably packed almost as many orders as I have and she has done all my bookkeeping for years. My father used to wash dishes, sweep the bakery, and run errands. For years my parents took care of Julie and Katie on Saturdays while we worked. A million thanks to them. Not to mention all the help my mother has given me with this book.

Then comes Paul, the love of my life, my best friend, and husband of thirty-five years. He has never left my side. When he worked at Fraser Morris he would make my deliveries before work. He has made countless extra trips for me. Stayed late with me to finish things. He is my biggest supporter, and he loves almost everything I bake. I couldn't ask for a better companion. I love you so much.

My boss at Fraser Morris, Eric Rosenthal, for his incredible generosity. He built me a beautiful baking space at Fraser Morris and when I left he gave me so much. He helped make Margaret Palca Bakes a reality.

Willy, for giving me the opportunity to taste the greatest Grand Marnier soufflé ever. Russel Carr for his expertise—if only I could have learned how to make tiny roses like he made.

Thank you, Tom Allen, for those great sandwiches you brought me in the hospital after both our daughters were born.

Patti, Tom, and Kip Hinsdale for their enthusiastic love of rugelach.

My first employee, Marcia Bishop—such a solid worker, and such a nice human being. Charlie Sahadi, my hero as a business man and wonderful person. If more people were like you this world would be so much better. You helped me so much in the beginning of my career—I will never forget.

Patsy Blackman, so important in our new kitchen on President Street. We had fun. I always think of the Spiegel catalogue days.

My two youngest workers, Eric Fisher and Winston German. Eric used to come after school to wash dishes for us. He is my first son. I love you, Eric, and thank you for your hard work.

Jermale McColley, my second son. Twenty years we've been doing this! I'll never forget the night at 191—I am forever grateful. You always have my heart.

Sarah Solis, thank you so much for sticking by me all these years.

Ryan Jones, such a nice fellow and good worker. The ice cream sandwich label is my favorite—I'm glad our paths crossed.

Ellie D'Eustachio for all your hard work on the website and potential books and such good work behind the counter! Glad I know you!

St. John Jordan dancing with the mop—every job was fun.

All the people who have worked for me over the years, too numerous to name. Present staff, Jose Mendes, and German Martinez! You make it possible.

Miguel Dionicio, nunca deja de hablar. Muchas Gracias!

Henry from Fall Café, colleagues in business, someone to commiserate with!

Muffin Spenser from 71, Claudio Martin from Mangia, Jose from Balducci, and Giacomo and Tanya from Grace's Marketplace. Peter and Ed! Yana from News Bar, Ted and Alan from Blue Apron, Gia and Peter from Farmacy, Jon from Corrado, Irwin and Kenny—thank you for all the butter! I always know it's Wednesday. Pearline and Michael from Valente, and Amanda Neil, the sweetest angel on the face of this earth, from Roots.

The invaluable recipe testers, Marie di Manno, Cynthia and Steve Harmon, Katy Zanville, and Hital Ohad Lipskin.

Kate Mellon, Marianne McKinney, and Sheila Gordon. I am so glad I met you and thank you for your patronage all these years. Marshall Sohne and the entire Sohne family, you keep the grill humming! So many loyal customers.

My brother Joe Palca always sending people my way.

Michael Harlan Turkell, photographer beyond compare, for his patience, generosity, and outstanding ability. Who could ask for more?

So much gratitude to my glitter expert—the gingerbread houses never looked better! Thank so much, Rebecca Kaplan.

Finally, Julie and Katie, my beautiful daughters. This book is for you. It is my gift to you. I missed a lot but I love you more than anything in the world. This part of me you will have forever.

INDEX

CONVERSION CHARTS

METRIC AND IMPERIAL CONVERSIONS
(These conversions are rounded for convenience)

Ingredient	Cups/Tablespoons/Teaspoons	Ounces	Grams/Milliliters
Butter	1 cup = 16 tablespoons = 2 sticks	8 ounces	230 grams
Cheese, shredded	1 cup	4 ounces	110 grams
Cream cheese	1 tablespoon	0.5 ounce	14.5 grams
Cornstarch	1 tablespoon	0.3 ounce	8 grams
Flour, all-purpose	1 cup/1 tablespoon	4.5 ounces/0.3 ounce	125 grams/8 grams
Flour, whole wheat	1 cup	4 ounces	120 grams
Fruit, dried	1 cup	4 ounces	120 grams
Fruits or veggies, chopped	1 cup	5 to 7 ounces	145 to 200 grams
Fruits or veggies, pureed	1 cup	8.5 ounces	245 grams
Honey, maple syrup, or corn syrup	1 tablespoon	0.75 ounce	20 grams
Liquids: cream, milk, water, or juice	1 cup	8 fluid ounces	240 milliliters
Oats	1 cup	5.5 ounces	150 grams
Salt	1 teaspoon	0.2 ounce	6 grams
Spices: cinnamon, cloves, ginger, or nutmeg (ground)	1 teaspoon	0.2 ounce	5 milliliters
Sugar, brown, firmly packed	1 cup	7 ounces	200 grams
Sugar, white	1 cup/1 tablespoon	7 ounces/0.5 ounce	200 grams/12.5 grams
Vanilla extract	1 teaspoon	0.2 ounce	4 grams

OVEN TEMPERATURES

Fahrenheit	Celsius	Gas Mark
225°	110°	¼
250°	120°	½
275°	140°	1
300°	150°	2
325°	160°	3
350°	180°	4
375°	190°	5
400°	200°	6
425°	220°	7
450°	230°	8